101
DEFENSIVE BACK
DRILLS

Ron Dickerson Sr.
James A. Peterson

ISBN: 1-57167-089-0
Library of Congress Catalog Card Number: 96-72471

Book Layout : Antonio J. Perez
Cover Design and Diagrams: Deborah M. Bellaire
Front cover photo: Jerry Millevoi

Coaches Choice Books is an imprint of: Sagamore Publishing, Inc.
                                             P.O. Box 647
                                             Champaign, IL 61824-0647
                                             (800) 327-5557
                                             (217) 359-5940
                                             Fax: (217) 359-5975
                                             Web Site: http//www.sagamorepub.com

DEDICATION

To my deceased grandparents,

Raymond and Gertrude Dickerson;

also to my role model,

the late Reverend Martin Luther King Jr.

ACKNOWLEDGMENTS

With the deepest appreciation I acknowledge the encouragement and assistance of the following people who read my manuscript in its early stages and made invaluable suggestions—my son, Ron Dickerson, Jr., my daughter, Rashawn Dickerson, Dr. Jim Peterson, Greg Shiano, Mrs. Shar Marbury, every ball player that I ever coached, and to the many young, persistent high school coaches who have learned from my coaching style.

The project was born from the constant encouragement of my wife, Jeannie. I give her and all the others my boundless thanks.

God is good, All the time: All the time, God is good.

—Ron Dickerson Sr.

CONTENTS

For the more than three decades that I have been playing and coaching football at the collegiate level, I have coaching and observing defensive backs. Collectively, my experiences have given me an opportunity to evaluate many techniques and fundamentals for playing defensive back and a variety of methods for teaching those techniques and fundamentals. In the process, I have come to realize that true learning occurs when there is a need to know, a solid understanding of how to learn exists, and coaches and players realize that a particular goal can be reached.

I wrote this book to provide football coaches at all competitive levels with a tool that can enable them to maximize the skills and attributes of their players. As a vehicle for teaching and learning, properly designed drills can have extraordinary value. *101 Defensive Back Drills* features drills that I have collected, field-tested, and applied over the course of my coaching career. If in the process of using the drills presented in this book, coaches are better able to develop the skills of the defensive backs, then the effort to write *101 Defensive Back Drills* will have been well worthwhile.

—Ron Dickerson Sr.

CHAPTER 1

WARM-UP DRILLS

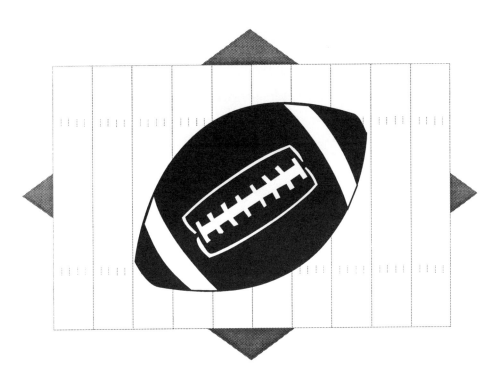

DRILL #1: MOVE AND REACT

Objective: To warm-up; to improve reaction time; to enhance stamina.

Equipment Needed: A football.

Description: The coach has the defensive backs spread out in several lines facing him. Each player is at least double-arms length from the closest player to him. With the ball in hand, the coach moves the ball one of four basic directions (left, right, forward and backward). The team responds to the movement of the ball and vigorously moves in the direction dictated by the coach. The coach also has the option of commanding the players to either run in place or to hit the ground by ordering them to "get on your face" or "get on your back". Both commands are quickly followed by an order to "get on your feet." The coach combines the directional movement commands with the various hit-the-ground commands to create a rigorous, non-stop warm-up session.

Coaching Points:

- The coach should require his players to respond to a new command every four to five seconds.

- When running in place, players should be required to lift their knees as high as possible.

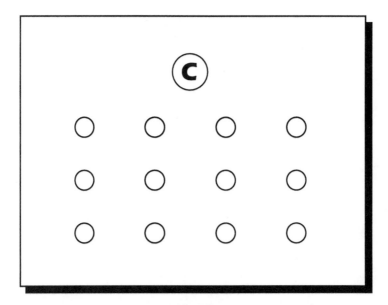

DRILL #2: JUMP AND TWIST

Objective: To warm-up; to enhance flexibility and balance.

Equipment Needed: None.

Description: The coach has the defensive backs straddle yard lines about three yards between each other, while assuming a good defensive position. The players should all be facing the coach in the 12 o'clock position. On the command, "Switch," the players jump about four inches off the ground, keep their feet spread and then twist their hips so that they are facing in the opposite direction. Upon landing on the ground, the players should again be straddling a yard line, facing away from the coach, this time at the 6 o'clock position. On the next command, "Switch," the players again jump, twist their hips and land straddling the yard line in the opposite direction. Each time the players jump, the jump should be away from the coach. The drill should be continued until the players have made six change of directions. At that time, the players should return to the point where they started and repeat the drill.

Coaching Points:

- The coach should require his players to maintain good balance and continue to straddle the yard line each time their feet come in contact with the ground.

- As players improve their performance, the coach can increase the cadence (i.e., frequency) of the "Switch" command.

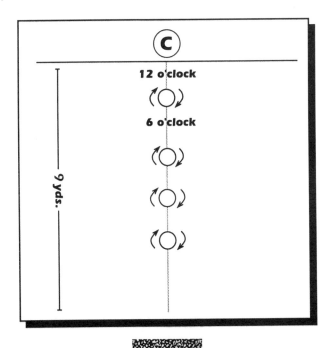

DRILL #3: RUN AND TWIST

Objective: To warm-up; to increase hip flexibility.

Equipment Needed: None.

Description: The coach has the players form three to five lines. The players face the coach, while keeping two to three yards from each other. On the command, "Go," the players in one line start back pedaling and twisting their hips as fast as they can. At the command, "Recover," the players stop and return to their starting position. While they are recovering, the coach gives the command, "Go," to the next line of players and continues in like manner, until each line has done the drill at least four times. Players in each line should back-pedal at least 20 yards before the coach asks them to recover.

Coaching Points:

- The coach should require the players to back-pedal and twist their hips at a moderate speed to start the drill. Once the players have warmed-up, they should increase their running and hip twisting speed.

- The players should run when recovering to the starting position in order to accentuate the warm-up benefits of the drill.

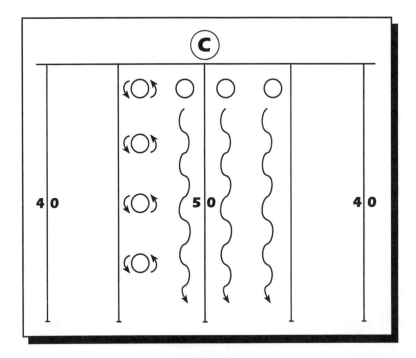

DRILL #4: TORSO/HIP TWISTER

Objective: To warm-up the player's torso, hips and legs.

Equipment Needed: None.

Description: The coach has the defensive backs form two lines facing each other, double-arms length distance between players. The distance between lines should be about 3-4 yards. To start the drill, one player assumes a defensive stance at one end of the two lines and in the middle between the two lines. On the coach's command, "Go," the player runs backward between the lines while twisting his torso to facilitate looking alternately over his right and then his left shoulder in order to keep from running into one of the lines. When he is about half-way down the lines, the next player in line should assume the starting position. The coach should start the next player as soon as the other player reaches the end of the lines. The players standing in the lines should cheer and clap and push the player running the drill back to the center if he runs into one of the lines.

Coaching Points:

- The coach should require the defensive backs to increase their speed running the drill as they become more proficient a performing the drill.

- The defensive backs should twist their torso and hips continually as they run the drill in order to obtain the maximum warm-up benefit from the drill.

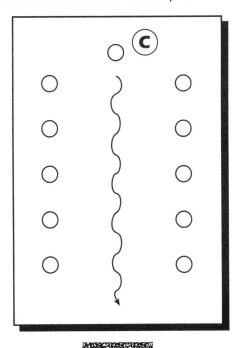

DRILL #5: HIGH CHOPS

Objective: To provide a pre-practice warm-up; to enhance foot and lateral quickness.

Equipment Needed: A football.

Description: The coach has all of the defensive backs form three lines, double-arms distance apart, facing him. The coach holds the football out in front of him. The drill begins when the coach slaps the ball, which is a signal to the first player in each line to jump forward and take up a good defensive stance. When the coach slaps the ball twice, the three players start to run in place, lifting their legs as high as possible and pumping their arms vigorously. The coach then starts to move the football to his right and to his left—slowly at first, then increasing his speed as the drill progresses. The players respond to the movement of the ball by shuffling laterally, as they continue to pump their arms and legs. The coach should continue the drill for about 15 - 20 seconds, then slap the football three times. The coach then points the ball in the direction he wants the players to break. The coach then slaps the ball one time, which is a signal to the next three players in line to jump out.

Coaching Points:

- The coach should require the players to keep lifting their legs as high as possible while continuing to pump their arms.

- As the players warm-up, the coach can increase the speed at which he moves the players laterally, as well as the duration of the drill.

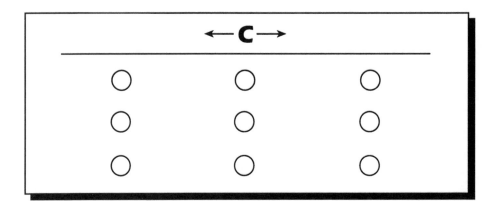

DRILL #6: HIGH KNEE ROPES

Objective: To warm-up prior to a full practice; to evaluate and enhance agility and quickness.

Equipment Needed: High knee ropes.

Description: A number of drills exist which involve use of high knee ropes. Among the examples of some the high knee rope drills are the following: require the players to run through by stepping in each opening or every other opening; cross-over using every opening or every other opening; hop straddle every opening or every other opening; high chops sideways using both feet every opening (start this action from outside of the ropes); use only the diagonals; perform laterals down and back; etc. The coach should plan a sequence of different methods of going through the high knee ropes for each session on the equipment.

Coaching Points:

- The coach can use the high knee ropes frequently in practice, but he should change the sequence of the drill each time in order to add variety to the drill. This approach will enhance the possibility of improving the players' level of quickness and agility.

- These various drills can be used by the coach as a diagnostic tool to determine which players possess an appropriate level of agility and quickness to play defensive back.

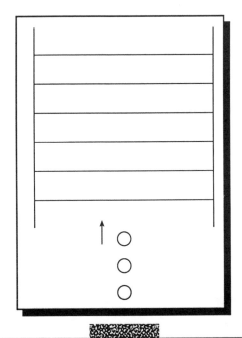

DRILL #7: THE BULL IN THE RING

Objective: To warm-up the players' muscles and joints; to increase players' enthusiasm prior to a game or practice.

Equipment Needed: None.

Description: The players form a circle around one player, who is acting as the "bull" in the ring. The bull moves around the *inside* of the circle, generating enthusiasm verbally and by feigning attacks. The bull attacks any player he desires (or the coach can control the bull's selection of a "target" by pointing to a player) After good sharp pad-to-pad contact is made with 3-4 different players, the coach assigns a different player to be a "bull". This drill should be continued until all players have been in the center of the ring.

Coaching Points:

- The attacking bull should not be allowed to repeatedly attack or take advantage of an obviously weaker opponent.

- The coach can help develop enthusiasm while warming up his players if he requires that this drill be executed properly and zealously.

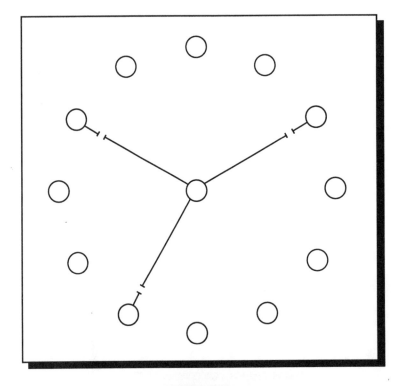

CHAPTER 2

QUICKNESS DRILLS

DRILL #8: LATERAL SHUFFLE

Objective: To develop foot quickness; to improve footwork.

Equipment Needed: None.

Description: The coach has the players form several lines with their toes on the yard lines, the players about three yards between each other. On the coach's command, "Right", the players shuffle to their right while alternating placing their left foot, then their right foot a comfortable distance in front of the yard line. Players should always have one foot on the yard line, with their other foot in front of the line as they shuffle laterally. After they have shuffled about 10 yards, the coach commands, "Left," which signals the players to reverse the direction of their shuffle. The players' foot movements should simulate jumping rope as they shuffle down the yard line.

Coaching Points:

- The coach should require the players to keep both feet moving while shuffling laterally as they would when skipping rope.

- As the players develop their skills in this drill, the coach should require the players to speed-up their shuffling movements in order to further enhance their level of foot quickness.

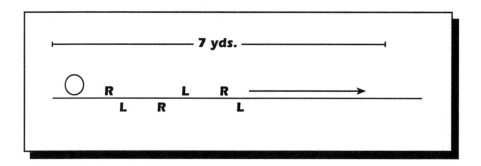

DRILL #9: BACK-PEDAL AND MOVE

Objective: To develop quickness in changing directions from the back-pedal; to develop aggressiveness in going for the ball.

Equipment Needed: A football.

Description: The coach has three defensive backs at a time assume a defensive position, arms distance apart, facing him. The coach then holds a football above his head with both hands. When the coach slaps the ball, the players start to back-pedal and attempt to reach full speed as quickly as possible. After the players reach full speed back-pedaling, the coach moves the football to indicate in which direction the players should move next. Moving the football straight back indicates the players should move directly forward; moving the football directly left or right means the players should break at a ninety degree angle in the direction indicated; and moving the football back at a 45-degree angle mean the players should move forward at a 45-degree angle. After each change of direction, the coach should have the players attain full speed, then slap the ball again to have them revert back to back-pedaling. After about 30 seconds of this drill, the coach should throw the football toward the center of the three players. All three players should go for the ball. At that point, the next three defensive back in line should get set to engage in the drill.

Coaching Points:

- The coach should require the players to attain full speed while they are back-pedaling in order to develop quickness in changing directions at top speed.

- The coach should require the players to attain top speed as quickly as possible after each change in direction to practice accelerating in all directions.

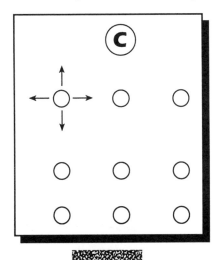

DRILL #10: BACK-PEDAL AND TWIST OUT

Objective: To develop quickness in changing directions or twisting while back-pedaling to accelerating in a straight line direction; to develop aggressiveness in going for the ball.

Equipment Needed: A football.

Description: The coach has three defensive backs at a time assume a defensive stance, double-arms distance apart, facing him. The coach then holds a football over his head. When the coach slaps the ball, the players start back-pedaling, accelerating to top speed as soon as possible. After the players back-pedal for seven or eight yards, the coach moves the football to indicate which direction the players should move next. Moving the ball straight forward means the players should twist out of their back-pedal and run straight away from the coach; moving the ball to either side means the players should twist and run a straight line parallel to the coach. After the players run seven or eight yards straight ahead, the coach should command, "ball", and throw the football toward the center of the three players. The players should turn and run for the ball. Simultaneously, the next three players in line should get set to participate in the drill.

Coaching Points:

- The coach should require the players to twist out of their back-pedal as quickly as possible.

- The coach should require the players to accelerate in a straight line after they twist out of their back-pedal to reach top speed as soon as possible.

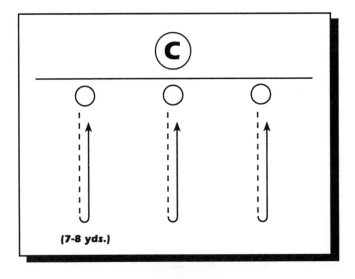

DRILL #11: BACK-PEDAL AND SLIDE

Objective: To develop quickness in changing directions and sliding side to side; to develop aggressiveness in going for the ball.

Equipment Needed: A football.

Description: The coach has four defensive backs at a time assume a low back-pedal position, double-arms distance apart, facing him. The coach then holds a football over his head. The coach starts the players back-pedaling by slapping the ball. After the players back-pedal about four yards, the coach moves the ball either to the right or to the left and the players slide (not cross-over) in that direction. After the players slide two or three yards, the coach slaps the ball again, indicating that the payers should again back-pedal. The coach should alternate left and right slides to keep the players in front of him. After about 30 seconds of the drill, the coach should throw the football toward the center of the payers. The players should all go for the ball. The next four players in line should get ready for the drill by jumping out in front of the coach and assuming the low back-pedal position.

Coaching Points:

- The coach should require the players to push off each time they change directions (square corners) and accelerate as quickly as possible.

- The coach should require the players to stay low and shuffle while moving. The coach should emphasize not using a cross-over step during the sidewards slide.

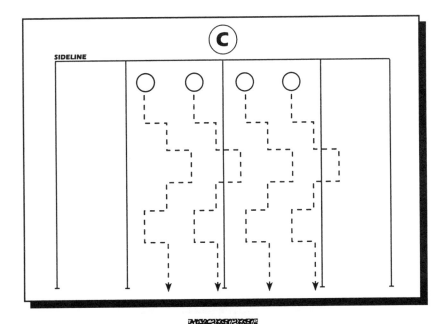

21

DRILL #12: LATERAL SHUFFLE

Objective: To develop quickness in moving laterally while keeping the shoulders square with the line of scrimmage and shuffling rather than using the cross-over while sliding sidewards; to improve hand-eye coordination.

Equipment Needed: A football.

Description: The coach has two players (A and B) standing on a line, five yards apart. The third player, C, stands next to player A. The coach holds a football in front of him and starts player C sliding from player A to player B by slapping the ball. When player C gets to the player B, he tags his elbow and then slides back to player A, tags his elbow and so on. After 30 seconds of the drill, the coach throws the football toward the sliding player, who tries to catch it. He then throws the ball back to the coach, and the players switch positions. The coach can have several groups of three doing this drill at the same time. In addition, he can alternate which group he throws the ball to when he wants to stop the drill to allow players to change positions.

Coaching Points:

- The coach should require the players to keep their shoulders square with the line of scrimmage throughout their slide and to refrain from using the cross-over step when sliding sidewards (the use of the lateral shuffle should be emphasized).

- The coach can increase the distance the players are required to slide in each direction after they become comfortable with this drill.

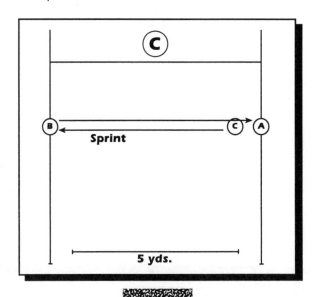

DRILL #13: ROPE JUMPING

Objective: To improve foot quickness; to enhance stamina.

Equipment Needed: Jump ropes.

Description: The coach should start his team jumping rope daily, having his players jump using two feet at a time for 10 to 15 minutes at a time for the first month. The players should be allowed to rest as needed. During the second month, the players should be required to jump rope on one leg for one minute, rest for 20 seconds, then repeat the sequence using the other leg. The drill should be continued for 15 minutes. At the start of the third month, the players should be required to alternate legs for each jump (skipping). The players should try to skip rope for 15 minutes non-stop, making as few mistakes as possible. Once the players have developed their skills at rope jumping/skipping, the length of the drill can be increased to at least 20 minutes.

Coaching Points:

- The coach should not expect players to progress quickly with this drill. Rope jumping is a skill that takes time for some players to master. The potential effect on foot quickness and balance, however, can make the effort involved worthwhile.

- This drill is aerobically demanding. As a result, coaches should allow their players to rest periodically (as needed) while they develop their aerobic capacity and rope-jumping skills.

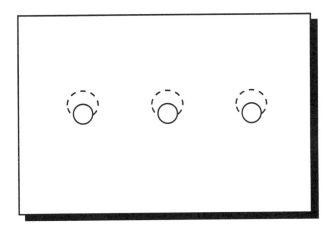

DRILL #14: QUARTER TURNS IN CADENCE

Objective: To improve foot quickness while executing turns in response to the quarterback calling signals.

Equipment Needed: None.

Description: The coach has three players at a time stand facing him, double-arms distance apart, ready to respond to the coach's (quarterback's) signal calling. When the coach calls "Set", the three players immediately assume a good defensive position, keeping low and facing the coach. When the coach calls, "Hike", the players turn to their right. The coach then calls "Set", and the players turn back to face the coach. When the coach call "Hike" again, the players turn first to their left, then back facing the coach again when he calls "Set". As the coach continues calling these signals for 15-20 seconds at a fast cadence, the players respond to his verbal cues. When the coach calls "Go", the players sprint from their positions in the direction the coach points. Simultaneously, the next three players take up positions to start the drill.

Coaching Points:

*   The coach should emphasize listening to the calls so that the players do not make any false movements or lose their poise.

*   The coach should require the players to execute turning movements in a precise manner with their shoulders square at all times. As the players become more proficient at this drill, the coach can speed up the cadence of his calls.

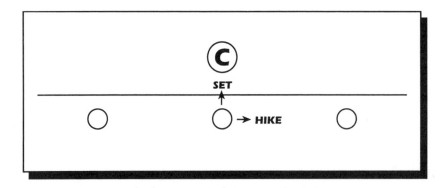

DRILL #15: QUICK AND CHOPPY

Objective: To develop foot quickness while executing the cross-over step.

Equipment Needed: None.

Description: The coach has three players at a time take positions along the sideline facing the middle of the field, double-arms distance apart. On the coach's command, the players should start running forward in a straight line while executing the cross-over step as rapidly a possible. The players should run in this manner from the sideline to the first hash mark, then cut left or right and return to the sideline. The next three players can take their starting positions as soon as the first three players start running and can start the drill when the players in front of them are half-way to the hash mark.

Coaching Points:

- The coach should require the players to run in a straight line while executing the cross-over step. The importance of maintaining good body balance should be stressed.

- As the players develop their skills in this drill, the coach should require the players to execute more cross-over steps and run faster.

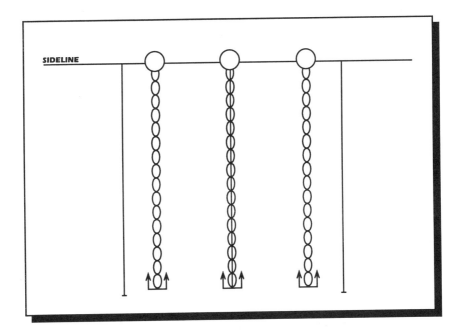

DRILL #16: AROUND THE CONE

Objective: To improve foot quickness.

Equipment Needed: Eight cones.

Description: The coach has the defensive backs form two lines similar to a relay race. Four cones—with two yards between each cone—should be placed five yards in front of each line. On the coach's command, the first player in each line sprints toward the cones. When he gets to each cone, he circles the cone, using very short, choppy steps, then continues to the next cone. After circling the last cone, the player back-pedals along the side of the cones to where the next player in line is waiting. The next player starts to run the drill when the player ahead of him passes the start point for the drill. The drill should continue until all players have had a chance to run it at least once. Competition between the groups in the form of relay races can add variety to this drill.

Coaching Points:

- The coach should require the players to circle the cones in a balanced, poised manner, using rapid choppy steps.

- As the players' level of conditioning improves, the coach could require each player to run the drill multiple times during each drill session.

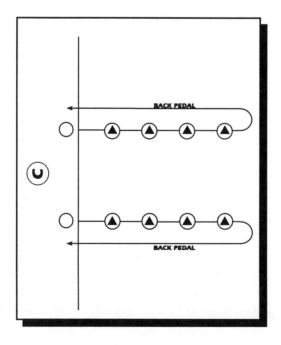

DRILL #17: AROUND THE BAG

Objective: To improve foot quickness and agility.

Equipment Needed: 16-20 stand-up blocking dummies.

Description: The coach has the defensive backs form two lines similar to a relay race. Five yards in front of each line, 8-10 blocking dummies are placed one yard apart. On the coach's command, the first player in each line sprints toward the dummies, then weaves through them as quickly as possible. When each player gets past the last dummy, he should back-pedal alongside the row of blocking dummies back to the starting position. The next player starts to run the drill when the player ahead of him back-pedals past the start point. The drill should continue until all players have had a chance to run it at least once. The coach could add competition to the drill by making it a relay race.

Coaching Points:

- The coach should emphasize the importance of planting a foot and pushing off in the new direction when the players are weaving through the blocking dummies.

- As the player's conditioning improves, the coach could require each player to run the drill multiple times during the drill session.

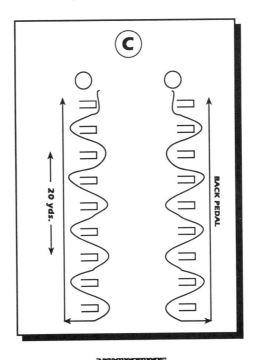

DRILL #18: THE JUGGLER

Objective: To improve the player's lateral quickness and timing; to enhance hand-eye coordination.

Equipment Needed: Two footballs.

Description: The coach starts this drill with a football in each hand and a player opposite him at a distance of 2-3 yards. The coach begins by tossing one ball toward the defensive back. The player catches the ball and throws it back to the coach. The coach then immediately throws the other ball to the player, making him move laterally in the opposite direction. This sequence is repeated until the coach or the defensive back drops the football.

Coaching Points:

- The defensive back must watch the coach's eyes and the football and must catch the ball using both hands.

- The coach should use this drill as a "change of pace" drill.

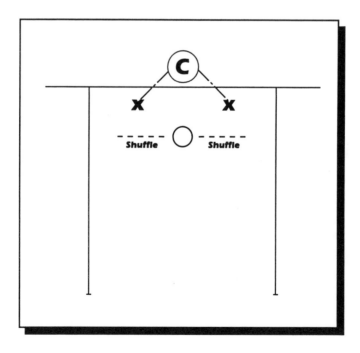

CHAPTER 3

MOVEMENT DRILLS

DRILL #19: BACK-PEDALING AND REACTION TO THE BALL

Objective: To improve maintenance of proper alignment with the line of scrimmage; to enhance back-pedaling techniques; to improve the ability to react to a thrown ball.

Equipment Needed: A football.

Description: The coach has four defensive backs spread out double-arms length, five yards in front and facing him. On the coach's command, "Set," the players assume a defensive stance. On the coach's command, "Go," the players start to back-pedal as when defending against a pass. After the players back-pedal for about ten yards, the coach should throw the football in the direction of one of the players. All four players should then react to the ball, trying to catch (intercept) the football. Players should maintain their proper alignment, keeping their eyes on the coach— ready to react to the ball. The drill should then be repeated with the next four defensive players.

Coaching Points:

- The coach should require his players to maintain proper alignment so as to keep their eyes on him at all times while they are back-pedaling.

- When the coach throws the football, players should be required to react to the ball quickly as though they were trying to intercept the pass.

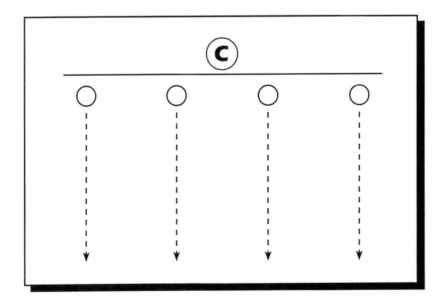

DRILL #20: KEEP LOW

Objective: To develop the defensive player's ability to keep low, with knees bent while shuffling to cover the receiver.

Equipment Needed: None

Description: The coach has the defensive backs spread out in several columns, double-arms length apart, facing him. The players should assume a bent-knee, relaxed defensive stance with one foot comfortably in front of the other (i.e., a staggered stance). On the coach's command, "Go," the players should push off with their back foot and continuing to move backward, alternately drag their left foot, then their right foot (shuffling) for about 10 yards. On the coach's command, "Recover," the players should sprint to the spot where they started and assume the same defensive position to start the drill again.

Coaching Points:

- The coach should emphasize that the players need to keep low while moving, with their knees bent, and use the shuffle to cover the receiver.

- The players should increase the speed at which they shuffle as they become comfortable with the drill. Once he has perfected the shuffle, a defensive back should be able to shuffle backward as fast as he can back-pedal, thereby adding to his ability to employ man-to-man coverage techniques.

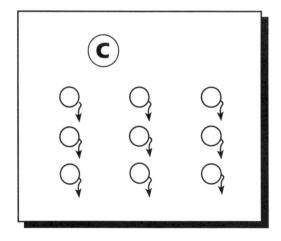

DRILL #21: WAVE

Objective: To develop the defensive player's ability to change facing directions (outside or inside) while back-pedaling.

Equipment Needed: None.

Description: The coach has three defensive backs assume a defensive stance, each straddling adjacent yard line (i.e., 45-50-45), and facing the coach. On the coach's command, "Go," the three players start to back-pedal down the line. The coach then points either to the left or to the right to have the players swing one of their legs across their body so that they are facing the direction he is pointing. The coach then points in the opposite direction which is a signal to the players to swing their opposite leg across their body to again face in the direction indicated by the coach. Throughout this drill the players should continue to back-pedal and maintain their balance. After the players have back-pedaled for about 15 yards, the coach commands, "Recover," and the players go to the end of the line. Simultaneously, the next three defensive backs take up positions facing the coach, ready to begin the drill.

Coaching Points:

* The coach should require the defensive backs to back-pedal in a straight line (stay on the yard line as much as possible) and maintain their balance.

* As the players become more comfortable with this drill, the coach should require them to change facing directions more frequently and back-pedal faster.

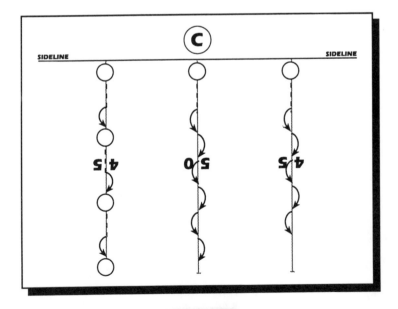

DRILL #22: BREAK AND CHURN

Objective: To enable defensive backs to develop the habit of continually moving their feet while changing their direction of movement.

Equipment Needed: None.

Description: The coach should have three defensive backs assume defensive positions, facing him, about double-arm distance apart. On the coach's command, "Go," the players start to back-pedal. After the players have moved about five yards, the coach commands, "Break," and the players break at a 45-degree angle in the direction the coach is pointing. After running about five yards in their new direction, the coach commands, "Recover," which signals the players to churn their feet while changing directions to run back as quickly as possible directly to where they started the drill.

Coaching Points:

- The coach should emphasize that defensive backs must develop the ability to change directions without planting or stopping their feet.

- As the players become more comfortable with this drill, the coach should require that they accelerate after each change of direction.

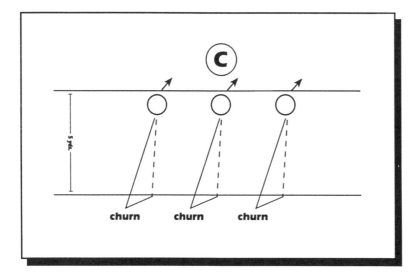

DRILL #23: BACK AND CHURN

Objective: To enable defensive backs to develop the habit of continually moving their feet while changing their direction of movement.

Equipment Needed: None.

Description: The coach has three defensive backs assume defensive positions, facing him, about double-arm distance apart. On the coach's command, "Go," the players start to back-pedal. After the players have gone about 10 yards, the coach commands, "Recover," which signals the players to churn their feet while changing directions to run back as quickly as possible directly to where they started the drill.

Coaching Points:

- The coach should emphasize that defensive backs need to develop the ability to change directions without planting or stopping the movement of their feet.

- As the players become more comfortable with this drill, the coach should require that they accelerate after the command, "Recover," and get back to the starting position as soon as they can.

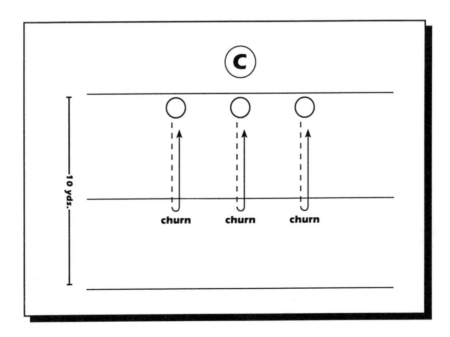

DRILL #24: TURN AND GO

Objective: To develop the ability of defensive backs to switch from back-pedaling to a straight-ahead sprint.

Equipment Needed: None.

Description: The coach has three defensive backs at a time assume defensive positions, double-arm distance apart, facing him. On the coach's command, "Go," the players start to back-pedal. The coach then commands either, "Left," "Right, " "Back, " "45-Right," or "Straight Ahead". After hearing the command, the players immediately twist out of back-pedaling, begin sprinting in the direction of the command given, and then accelerate for about five yards. The three players then recover, while the next three players assume defensive positions to start the drill. The coach should vary his command indicating the direction of the sprint so that all players get to experience moving in all directions.

Coaching Points:

- The coach should require the players to twist out of their back-pedaling and switch into a forward sprint as quickly as possible.

- As the players become more comfortable with this drill, they should be able to accelerate to their top speed during the forward sprint.

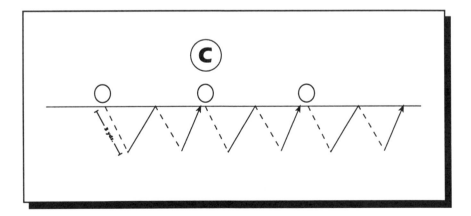

DRILL #25: T-STEP

Objective: To develop the ability to change directions (break on the ball) using the T-step technique.

Equipment Needed: A football.

Description: The coach has four defensive backs line up facing him, double-arm distance apart. Each player assumes a defensive stance. The coach then signals the players to start back-pedaling by dropping back (like a quarterback showing pass.) When the coach slaps the ball and faces either to the left or the right , the players should stop in such a manner that the position of their feet forms a "T". The base of the "T" should be pointing in the direction the coach is facing, while the foot forming the top of the "T" should be used to push off with to initiate a quick acceleration in the new direction. The coach should then throw the football toward the center of the players, who then converge on the ball and attempt to catch (intercept) it. The next three players then line up to engage in the drill.

Coaching Points:

- The coach should remember that not all players can perfect the "T-step " technique.

- The coach should emphasize bringing the foot that was the top of the "T" over the base foot in order to accelerate in the new direction. In addition, the arms and shoulders should be used (i.e., coordinated movement) to accentuate the effort to drive forward.

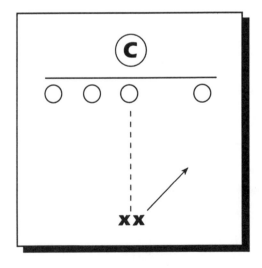

DRILL #26: DIAGONAL BACK-PEDAL

Objective: To improve footwork on turns; to develop the ability to maintain speed while running on a diagonal.

Equipment Needed: A football.

Description: The coach has the defensive backs form three lines and take up good defensive positions while straddling the yard lines five yards apart. All players should be facing the coach who is on the sideline. When the coach raises the football to show pass, all players should get set to react to the ball. The coach then moves the ball laterally, which is a signal to the players to back-pedal on a 45-degree angle in the direction the ball moves. After the players back-pedal about five to seven yards, the coach should move the ball in the other direction. The players should again react to the movement of the ball by pivoting and back-pedaling on a 45-degree angle in the direction the ball moved. Ultimately, the coach should have the players back-pedal four times in each direction. He should then throw the ball toward the center of the players. The players should react to the ball (i.e., attempt to intercept it) and then sprint to the sideline.

Coaching Points:

- The coach should require the players to execute a definite pivot for each change of direction, then accelerate in the new direction.

- As the players develop their skill at this drill, the coach should require the players to increase their speed both when back-pedaling and during the pivots when they change directions.

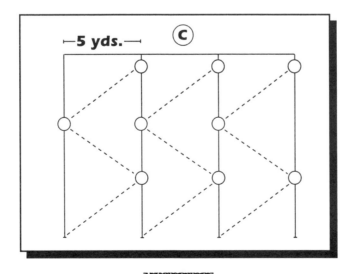

DRILL #27: QUARTER EAGLES

Objective: To improve foot speed while executing facing movements.

Equipment Needed: A football.

Description: The coach has three players at a time take up good defensive positions, double-arms distance apart, facing him. The coach holds the football in front of him to alert the players. He then moves the ball quickly to one side and then back to his front for a moment, then quickly to the other side, then to the front again. The players should react to the ball movement by executing left and right quarter turns as fast as the coach moves the ball. Then, the next three players should jump out and take up good defensive positions—prepared to perform the drill.

Coaching Points:

- The coach should require the players to shuffle their feet, to keep their shoulders square and to maintain good balance as they execute the left and right quarter turns.

- As the players develop their skill at this drill, the coach can increase the speed at which he moves the football. Also, as the player's level of conditioning improves, the length of the duration of this drill can be increased.

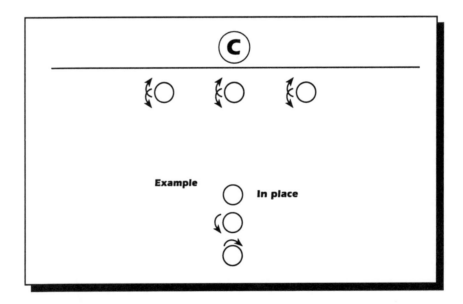

DRILL #28: CROSSING THE LINE

Objective: To improve agility, hip flexibility, and foot quickness.

Equipment Needed: None.

Description: The coach has the players form a single line, with the first player's toes on a yard line. On the coach's command, the first player starts to move laterally down the line by stepping diagonally forward in front of the line with his lead leg, then diagonally backward (cross-step) in back of the line with his trail leg. As soon as the first player moves five yards down the line, the next player should start the drill, and so on. The players should perform the drill from hash mark to hash mark.

Coaching Points:

- The coach should remind the players that this drill is designed to develop hip flexibility as well as agility and foot speed. The objective of this drill is not to work on player's lateral movement technique (lateral moves are done using the shuffle, not a cross-step).

- As the players develop their skills in this drill, the coach should require them to increase their speed of movement and take short, choppy steps.

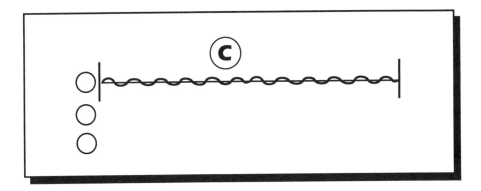

DRILL #29: BACK-PEDALING AND BREAKING AT 45 DEGREES

Objective: To improve the ability of a defensive back to move backwards, react to the football and intercept it.

Equipment Needed: A football.

Description: The coach faces one player at a time, who is positioned approximately 5-10 yards away. The coach starts the drill by moving the football sharply to the left or the right. The player reacts by moving backwards at a 45-degree angle in the same direction as the coach has moved the football. The player keeps his eye on the coach and the football. After 1-2 seconds, the coach moves the football in the opposite direction. The player reacts by immediately moving in the opposite direction, still at a 45-degree angle backwards. This sequence is repeated three to four times before the coach throws the football in the general direction of the defensive player. The player intercepts the football and returns the football to the coach by running back and handing it to him. (Many teams incorporate a team "callword," such as "BINGO," to let their teammates know that the ball has been intercepted.) This drill, which is often called the BINGO drill, requires the player to yell "BINGO" as he returns the ball to the coach.

Coaching Points:

- The player should start when the football moves. At that point, the player should stay low while back-pedaling, maintaining eye contact with the coach and changing directions quickly.

- The player should intercept the ball at the highest possible point, yell "BINGO" (or whatever codeword the coach desires) and then sprint the football back to the coach.

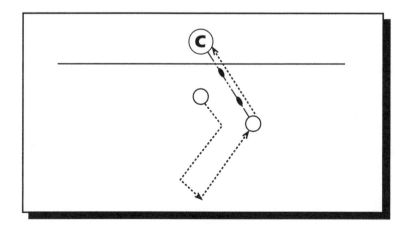

DRILL #30: BACK-PEDALING AND BREAKING AT 90 DEGREES

Objective: To improve the ability of a defensive back to move laterally, react to the football and intercept it.

Equipment Needed: A football.

Description: The coach faces one player at a time, who is positioned approximately 5-10 yards away. The coach starts the drill by commanding, "Set." When the player is in a good defensive stance, the coach commands, "Go." The player reacts by moving directly backwards. The player keeps his eyes on both the coach and the football. After 1-2 seconds, the coach moves the football to the right or left. The player reacts immediately by moving in the same direction as the football at a 90-degree angle laterally. The coach throws the football in the general direction of the defensive player. The player intercepts the football and returns the football to the coach by running back and handing it to him. (Many teams use a team "callword" such as "BINGO" to let their teammates know that the ball has been intercepted. This drill requires the player to yell "BINGO" as he returns the ball to the coach).

Coaching Points:

- The player should start moving quickly backwards when the coach commands "go." Staying low while back-pedaling, the player should maintain eye contact with the coach and change directions quickly.

- The player should intercept the ball at the highest possible point, yell "BINGO" (or whatever codeword the coach desires) and then sprint the football back to the coach.

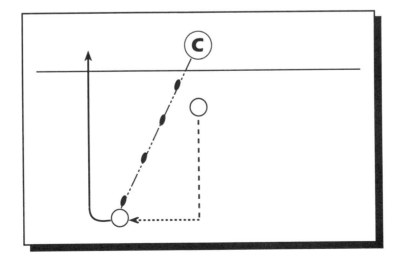

DRILL # 31: TURN AND GO

Objective: To improve the ability of a defensive back to back-pedal, turn and run, react to the football and intercept it.

Equipment Needed: A football.

Description: The coach faces one player at a time, who is positioned 1-2 yards away. The coach starts the drill by commanding, "Set." When the player is in a good defensive stance, the coach commands, "Go" (or by slapping the football). The player reacts by moving directly backwards, while keeping his eyes on the coach and the football. After several seconds, the coach commands, "Go." The player reacts immediately by turning and sprinting in the same direction as he has been moving (simulating catching up with an offensive receiver who is about to overtake him). The coach throws the football over the outside shoulder of the defensive player. The player intercepts the football, sprints forward toward the coach and returns the football to the coach, as that the next play can begin the next drill. Many teams use a team "callword," such as "BINGO," to let their teammates know that the ball has been intercepted. This drill can also be used to practice going from defense to offense rapidly by having the player yell "BINGO" as he returns the ball to the coach.

Coaching Points:

- The player should start moving quickly backwards when the coach commands, "Go." Staying low while back-pedaling, the player should maintain eyeball contact with the coach and turn to sprint on command or signal from the coach.

- The player should move toward the ball, intercept it at the highest possible point, yell "BINGO" (or whatever codeword the coach desires) and then sprint forward, handing the football back to the coach.

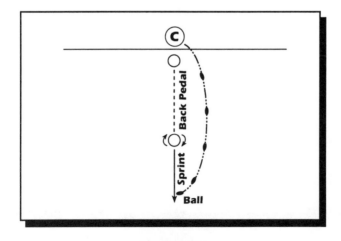

DRILL #32: RUN THE LINE

Objective: To improve the ability of a defensive back to pivot 190 degrees while running backwards, react to the football and intercept it.

Equipment Needed: A football.

Description: The coach faces one player at a time, who is positioned approximately 5-10 yards away. The coach starts the drill by commanding, "Go." The player reacts by moving directly backwards (180 degrees away from the coach). The coach then moves the football to the left or the right. The player reacts by planting his rear foot, dropping his butt, and using his *arms and hips to turn 180 degrees* in the opposite direction. After 1-2 seconds, while the player continues running backwards, the coach moves the football in the opposite direction. The player reacts immediately by turning his body 180 degrees while continuing to move straight backwards. This action is repeated three to four times before the coach throws the football in the general direction of the defensive player. The player intercepts the football and returns the football to the coach by running back and handing it to him.

Coaching Points:

- The player should start when the football moves. Staying low while running straight backwards, the player should always maintain eye contact with the coach and change directions quickly.

- The coach must stress that the player should use his arms and hips to help him rapidly turn his body 180 degrees.

- The player should intercept the ball at the highest possible point, yell "BINGO" (or whatever codeword the coach desires) and then sprint the football back to the coach.

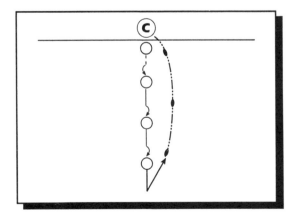

DRILL #33: DEFENSIVE BACK OBSTACLE COURSE

Objective: To develop footwork by requiring defensive backs to perform a series of maneuvers (e.g., back-pedaling, accelerating forward and backwards, hurdling, etc.); to assess the ability of defensive backs to perform a sequence of maneuvers within a specific time.

Equipment Needed: Six cones; four blocking dummies; two to four stop watches.

Description: The obstacle course is set up according to the layout illustrated in the diagram. The six cones are used to establish the boundaries of a 15-yard x 20-yard rectangular field. Two blocking dummies (one on top of the other) are stacked, slightly tilted in each of the two 15-yard x 10-yard areas created by the placement of the cones. The drill begins by having a player start with his heels on the line. On the coach's command, the first player to perform the drill back-pedals 15 yards, accelerates forward on a diagonal, hurdles the two stacked blocking dummies, and then accelerates forward and hits the front line. He then repeats the process in the second 15-yard x 10-yard area. He finishes the drill once he hits the front line again by exploding off and back-pedaling as fast as possible to the finish point. Once a player has reached the second cone, another player can start the drill.

Coaching Points:

- The importance of staying low and keeping the feet churning (i.e., never planted) should be emphasized.

- Players should be required to explode out of a backward or forward motion.

- An element of competitiveness can be added to the drill by having the player compare the time to complete the obstacle course against predetermined time standards (e.g., great = less than 15 secs; good = 15-17 secs; average = 17-19 secs; below average = more than 19 secs).

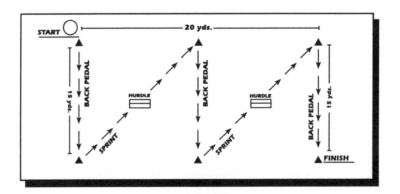

CHAPTER 4

REACTION DRILLS

DRILL #34: REACT AND GO

Objective: To enhance the ability of a defensive back to react to ball movement; to practice blitzing the quarterback.

Equipment Needed: A football; two cones or blocking dummies.

Description: The drill involves the coach and three players. Representing interior offensive linemen, two cones (or blocking dummies) are set up five yards apart on a yard line. Standing between the cones, the coach snaps the ball to an individual serving as a quarterback. On movement of the ball, the two defenders sprint low and hard across the line of scrimmage and converge on the quarterback who is positioned six yards behind the cones.

Coaching Points:

- The coach should use various kinds of cadence before snapping the ball in order to get the defensive backs used to reacting to the ball, as opposed to the "quarterback's" voice inflections. If necessary, a manager or an injured player can snap the ball.

- The coach should remind the defensive backs that their first priority is to key the football and sprint six yards.

- After each rep, the players should switch sides so they can attack from both sides, then flip sides.

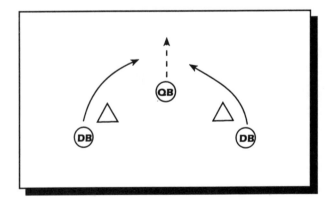

DRILL #35: REACH AND CATCH

Objective: To practice reacting to the snap of the football; to develop hand coordination and quickness; to enhance the ability of a defensive back to recover a fumble.

Equipment Needed: One (Nerf) football; two tennis balls.

Description: The drill involves two players, a coach, and someone to simulate a snap. As the ball is snapped, the players' eyes focus on the tennis balls that are being held by the coach who is positioned three yards from the football. The coach has his arms out from his body forming a "T." Players react to the dropping of the tennis ball by the coach and try to catch the ball before it hits the ground a second time. After all players go from a depth of three yards from the coach, the coach can move back to four yards, etc. A depth of five to six yards from the coach is considered especially challenging. The coach should be particularly alert once the competitive level of the drill is increased and players start diving for the tennis balls.

Coaching Points:

- Once the defensive backs become proficient at reacting to and going for the tennis balls, the coach could switch to using two actual footballs.

- The key is to focus on reacting to the snap of the ball and on moving quickly to catch the falling tennis ball.

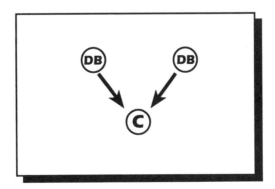

DRILL #36: REACT AND MIRROR

Objective: To enhance the ability of a defensive back to react to the actions of an offensive player; to develop the ability to move by sliding; to improve quickness; to warm-up.

Equipment Needed: A football; two blocking dummies.

Description: A ball carrier (BC) and a defensive back (DB) stand facing each other about four to five yards in front of a yard line between two blocking dummies placed on the ground approximately seven yards apart. The drill involves having the ball carrier attempt to cross the yard line between the two blocking dummies without being held up by the defender. The ball carrier moves laterally as quickly as possible and attempts to face the defender. The defender, mirroring the ball carrier, reacts to the movements of the ball-carrier and slides to stay in front of his opponent. His goal is to keep the ball carrier from scoring (i.e., crossing the yard line). The defender may use his hands, but the emphasis is on reacting quickly and moving his feet. The ball carrier has a specific time limit (e.g., 15 seconds) in which to score.

Coaching Points:

- The defenders must not be permitted to overextend their arms while using their hands on the ball carrier.

- To emphasize the need for a defender to move his feet, the drill can be performed by requiring the defender to keep his hands behind his back during the drill.

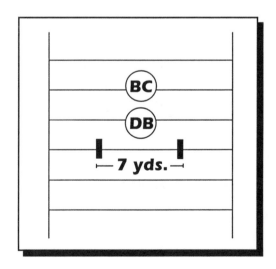

DRILL 37: REACT TO THE BALL

Objective: To enhance the ability of a defensive back to react to the ball; to develop hand and eye coordination while the defender is on the move.

Equipment Needed: A football.

Description: The drill involves having the defensive backs form one line about 20 yards from the coach, facing him. When the coach raises the football showing pass, the first player in line sprints toward the coach at top speed. When the player gets within 3-4 yards of the coach, the coach throws the football at the player's chest, requiring the player to react quickly to the ball and catch it before it hits him. After the player catches the ball, he tosses it back to the coach and returns to the back of the line. The coach then raises the football to signal the next player in line to start the drill and so on.

Coaching Points:

- The coach should emphasize the importance of watching the ball and reacting to it once it is thrown.

- The coach can add variety to this drill by throwing the football either over the player's head or below the player's waist, thereby, requiring the defender to play the ball at unusual angles.

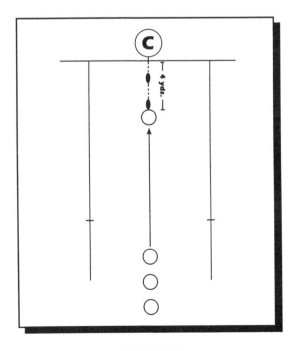

DRILL 38: BREAK TO THE BALL

Objective: To enhance the ability of a defensive back to react to the ball; to develop hand and eye coordination; to practice moving to the football.

Equipment Needed: A football.

Description: The drill involves having the defensive backs form one line about 20 yards from the coach, facing him. When the coach raises the football showing pass, the first player starts to sprint directly toward the coach. When the player gets within 10 yards of the coach, the coach pumps his arm like faking a pass toward the side he wants the player to break. The player should then break at a 90-degree angle to that side. Once the player makes his break, the coach should throw the football at the player to make him react quickly to catch the ball. The player should then return the ball to the coach and return to the end of the line. The coach then raises the football to signal the next player in line to start the drill, and so on.

Coaching Points:

- The coach should emphasize that players should watch the football at all times, especially as they try to catch it.

- To add variety to this drill, the coach can throw the football in front of or behind the defender in order to make him react to the ball at various, different angles.

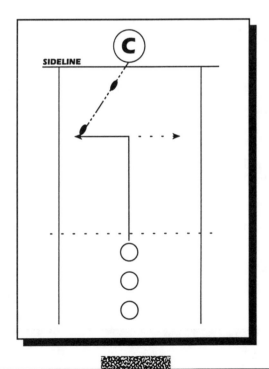

CHAPTER 5

STAMINA
DRILLS

DRILL #39: CATCH-ME-IF-YOU-CAN

Objective: To improve stamina; to warm-up.

Equipment Needed: None.

Description: The coach has the entire defensive team spread out in three lines on the field facing him. One group is on the goal line, while the other two groups are on the 10-yard and the 20-yard line respectively. On the coach's command, the players run ten yards and touch the line, retreat five yards and touch the line, run forward again for ten yards and touch the line, sprint backwards again for five yards and touch the line, etc. The process is repeated until the entire team has run the length of the field. The defensive backs (DBs) should start at the goal line, the linebackers (LBs) on the 10-yard line, and the defensive line (DL) on the 20-yard line. The players should be positioned (i.e., handicapped) according to their role on the team.

Coaching Points:

- If one particular group of defenders (DL's or LB's) needs a greater handicap, the coach can increase the distance between groups.

- The coach can incorporate competition into the drill by requiring any player who is passed by someone in one of the lines behind him to perform some arbitrary number of push-ups.

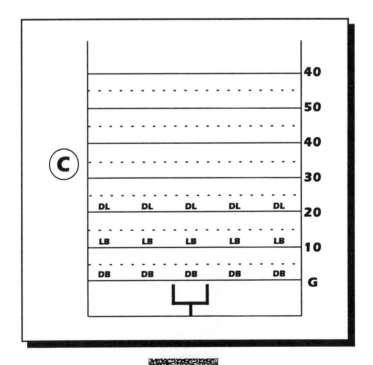

DRILL #40: AROUND THE WORLD

Objective: To enhance stamina; to improve footwork; to warm-up.

Equipment Needed: None.

Description: The drill involves three defensive backs at a time who line up on a yard line to the left of a hash mark. On command from the coach, the players sprint forward 20 yards, then shuffle to their right to the other hash mark, then backpedal back to the original starting line, and then shuffle left back to their original starting point. While they are moving, the coach has the option of having the players either run in place or hit the ground by ordering them to "Get on your face" or "Get on your back." Both commands should be quickly followed by the order to "Get on your feet and move—which is a signal for the players to resume their "around-the-world" route at top speed. The route, combined with the various hit-the-ground and run-in-place commands, is designed to create a rigorous, non-stop, warm-up session.

Coaching Points:

- All movements should be done at top speed, without hesitation.

- When running in place, players should be required to lift their knees as high as possible.

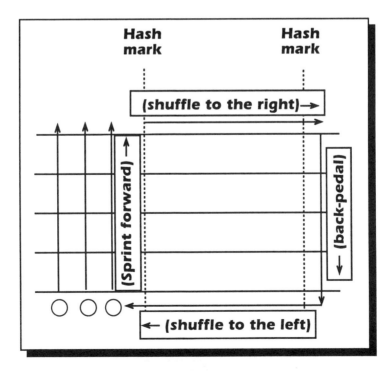

DRILL #41: PIKE'S PEAK

Objective: To develop stamina; to practice lateral movements; to enhance lateral quickness; to warm-up.

Equipment: Nine cones or scrimmage vests.

Description: The coach places nine cones (or scrimmage vests) in a dispersed manner on successive yards lines over a distance of 45 yards. The lateral distance between the cones decreases gradually as the cones are positioned further from the first cone. The drill begins with the defensive backs lining up behind the first cone. On command from the coach, the first player in line runs around the outside of each cone as fast as he can and sprints the last cone. The coach times the player's run. The rest of the defenders in line yell and shout encouragement to the player performing the drill. After the player completes the run, he goes to the end of the line. The next defender then runs the "Pike's Peak" layout.

Coaching Points:

- Each defender should be encouraged to cut the corners sharply on the run and go all-out until he sprints past the last cone.

- The coach can add an element of competition to the drill by establishing a minimum time for completing the run. Players who fail to make the minimum time can be required to perform a predetermined number of push-ups, sprints, etc.

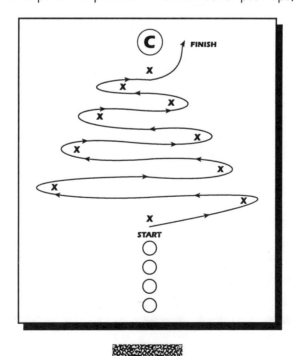

DRILL #42: STAGGER-SPURT

Objective: To develop stamina; to improve footwork; to practice changing directions quickly; to warm-up.

Equipment Needed: Twelve cones or scrimmage vests.

Description: The coach lays out 12 cones (or scrimmage vests), dispersed as shown, over a distance of 40 yards. The drill begins by having the defensive backs line up behind the first cone. On command from the coach, the first player in line sprints forward for ten yards, then back-pedals for five yards. He then turns and repeats the sequence over the next two cones (sprinting forward for ten yards and back-pedaling five yards). The defender completes the course by performing four additional, similar sequences. A complete run through the "stagger-spurt" layout involves sprinting forward for 55 total yards and back-pedaling for 25 yards. Once a player has reached the midway point in the layout, the next player in line should begin performing the drill.

Coaching Points:

- The coach should emphasize the importance of an all-out effort during the run and the value of changing directions quickly.

- The coach can add an element of competition to the drill by timing each player's run. Players who fail to perform the run "fast enough" can be required to do an arbitrary number of push-ups, sprints, etc.

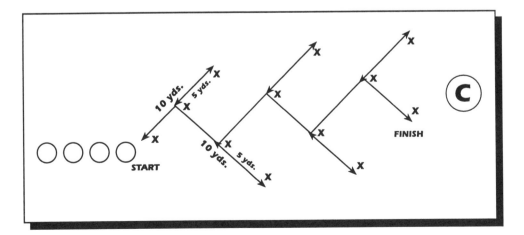

DRILL #43: BACK-PEDAL DUCK WADDLE

Objective: To develop stamina in the upper leg; to loosen up the hips and knees; to warm-up.

Equipment Needed: None.

Description: The coach has the defensive backs spread out in front of him. The players should assume a stance which involves an exaggerated level of flexion in their hips and knees (i.e., squat like a duck). On command, the players back-pedal at half speed, while maintaining their flexed "duck-like body position."

Coaching Points:

- Players should be encouraged to stay off their heels while participating in the drill.

- The coach should emphasize to the players that they should keep their head, arms, and pads in a game-like position during the drill.

- As the players become more comfortable in their ability to perform this drill, the coach can increase either the speed at which the players must back-pedal or the distance they're required to travel.

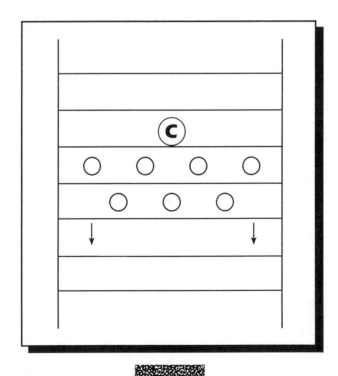

DRILL #44: AROUND THE DUMMIES

Objective: To improve stamina; to warm-up; to improve the ability of a defensive back to change directions quickly while moving laterally.

Equipment Needed: A minimum of four blocking dummies.

Description: The blocking dummies are placed on the ground parallel to each other as illustrated in the diagram. The coach assumes a position at one end of the row of blocking dummies. The defender begins in a position just outside to the left of the first bag, facing toward the coach. On a signal from the coach, the defender slides or runs laterally between the blocking dummies at an approximately a 45-degree angle. When he reaches the outside of the next blocking dummy, the defender pivots back to the inside (while continuing to face the coach). The drill continues non-stop in the same manner. After the defender reaches the last blocking dummy, he sprints forward for five yards at full speed.

Coaching Point:

- Competition can be added to the drill by having groups of players compete against each other in relay fashion.

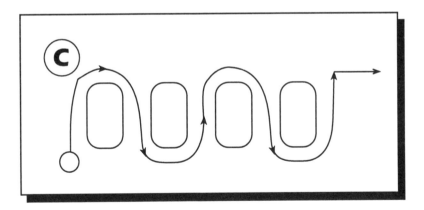

DRILL #45: CHANGE OF DIRECTION RACES

Objective: To improve stamina; to improve the ability of a defensive back to change directions quickly; to warm-up.

Equipment Needed: None.

Description: The defenders stand facing the coach with their near foot placed on a yard line. On a signal from the coach (C), the defenders run laterally until they touch the adjacent yard line (five yards away). While the defenders are moving, they must keep their shoulders square to the coach. After touching the opposite line, the defenders quickly change directions and run laterally back to the initial starting line. The drill continues until each defender has run six round-trips (a total distance of 60 yards). The drill is then repeated with the players facing the opposite direction.

Coaching Point:

- Variety can be added to the drill by having the defenders stand on the yard line, facing the opposite line, with their shoulders parallel to the line. On a command from the coach, the defenders sprint forward five yards and touch the next yard line. They then run backwards and touch the initial starting line. The drill continues until each defender has completed at least six round trips (a total of 60 yards).

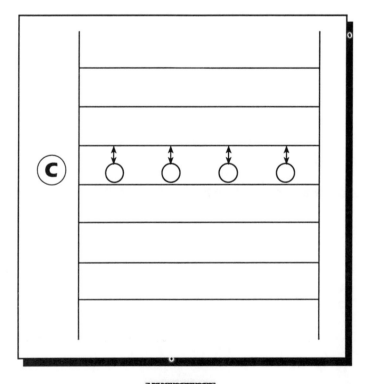

DRILL #46: DOUBLE MIRROR

Objective: To improve stamina; to develop the ability of a defensive back to change directions while running either backwards or laterally; to warm-up.

Equipment Needed: None.

Description: The defenders position themselves as illustrated, facing the coach (C). The coach signals the closest defender to him to move. That defender is commanded to perform one of three basic movements—run backwards in a straight line, run laterally at a 45-degree angle, or run forward in a straight line. The other three defenders mirror the movements of the first player, all the while maintaining the same distance between each other. On a final signal from the coach, all of the defenders sprint full speed past the coach.

Coaching Point:

- The drill is designed to enable defenders to respond to two stimuli simultaneously.

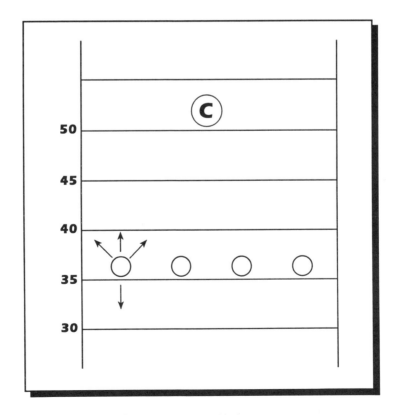

DRILL #47: GASSERS

Objective: To develop stamina; to improve the ability of a defensive back to change directions quickly; to improve the footwork involved in back-pedaling.

Equipment Needed: None

Description: The defenders line up on the goal line, three-four yards apart, facing the coach who is positioned on the 50-yard line. On a signal from the coach, the players simultaneously sprint to the five-yard line and then back-pedal as fast as they can back to the goal line. As quickly as possible, the defenders again sprint forward— this time to the ten-yard line. They then back-pedal to the goal line. Increasing the distance the players must sprint five yards at a time, the (sprint-back-pedal) sequence continues until the players have reached the mid-field yard line.

Coaching Points:

- Variety can be added to the drill by having the players either sprint or back-pedal in both directions.

- Competition can be fostered between players by having the coach time the drill.

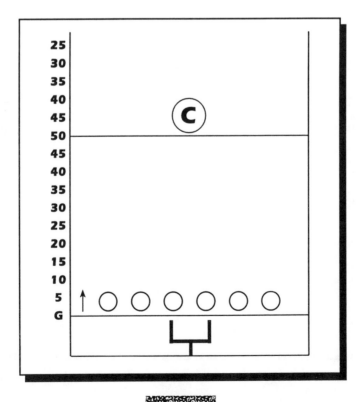

CHAPTER 6

TACKLING DRILLS

DRILL #48: THE TWO-MAN HIT AND BOUNCE

Objective: To improve the ability of a defensive back to "front-up" a ball carrier; to warm-up the muscles and joints prior to full-scale, live tackling drills.

Equipment Needed: A football.

Description: The drill involves placing the players in groups of three. One player acts as a ball carrier, while the other two serve as tacklers. The coach positions the two tacklers centered-on and opposite the ball-carrier at a distance of about 3 4 yards. The drill begins when the coach pitches the ball to the ball-carrier, who then runs at one of the defenders. The defensive back gets into a good hitting position and "fronts-up" the runner without tackling him. The defender's hit on the ball-carrier causes the ball-carrier to bounce backwards 3-4 yards. The ball-carrier then approaches the other defender who also gets into a good tackling position and strikes an effective blow, but allows the runner to escape. This sequence continues until the runner has been hit "properly" 2-3 times per tackler. At that point, the coach then blows his whistle and rotates the offensive defensive players.

Coaching Points:

* The defensive back should keep his head up and his eyes open while simultaneously sticking his face in the runner's numbers.

* The coach should review all basic tackling fundamentals. The defender should wrap-up the ball-carrier without tackling him, bend his knees and strike a blow without running through the ball carrier.

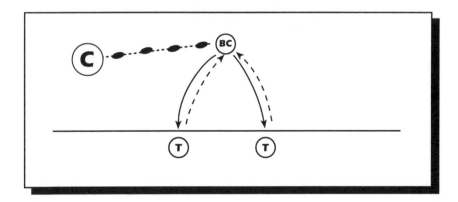

DRILL # 49: THE THREE-MAN HIT AND BOUNCE

Objective: To improve the ability of a defensive back to "front-up" a ball carrier; to warm-up the muscles and joints prior to full-scale live tackling drills.

Equipment Needed: A football.

Description: The drill involves placing the players in groups of four. One player acts as a ball-carrier, while the other three defenders serve as tacklers. The coach positions the three tacklers centered on and opposite the ball-carrier at a distance of about 3-4 yards. The drill begins when the coach pitches the ball to the ball-carrier who then runs between two of the defenders. The defenders both step into the runner without tackling him. The resultant collision causes the ball-carrier to bounce backwards 3-4 yards. The ball-carrier then approaches the gap between the other two defensive backs. They also assume a good tackling position and strike a forceful blow, but allow the runner to escape. This drill should continue until the runner has been bounced backwards 2-3 times. At that point, the coach then blows his whistle, stops the hitting and has the players rotate.

Coaching Points:

- The defenders should keep their heads up and their eyes open, while stepping into the ball-carrier with their inside shoulder (that shoulder which is closest to the runner at time of impact).

- The coach should review all basic tackling fundamentals. The defenders should strike a blow without tackling, bend their knees and step into (without running through) the ball-carrier.

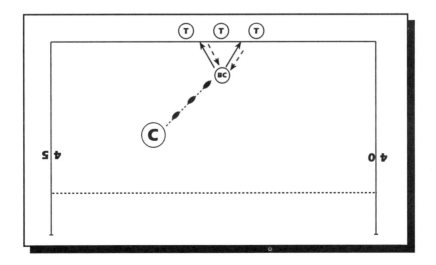

DRILL #50: FORM TACKLING

Objective: To improve the players' ability to tackle without being injured; to warm-up the muscles and loosen joints; to increase player enthusiasm prior to live drills or a game.

Equipment Needed: None.

Description: The players will face each other on opposite sides of a yard line, approximately 2-3 yards apart. They should be paired opposite someone of fairly equal height and weight. One line should be designated as ball carriers, while the opposite line serves as tacklers. On command from the coach, each tackler should pick up the ball carrier opposite him and carry him backwards 2-3 yards and set him down on the ground on his feet. (This drill is best done at 50-75% of full speed). After each repetition, the roles of the players should be switched.

Coaching Points:

- A perfect-heads up, eyes open, neck-bowed tackle should be the goal of each tackler.

- Variety can be added to this drill by having the players tackle at a 45-degree angle, instead of head-on.

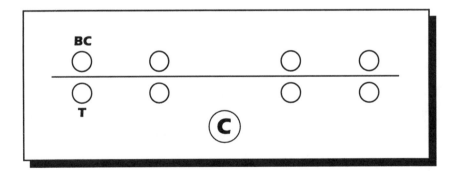

DRILL #51: THE POPSICLE STICK-DRIVE

Objective: To improve the player's ability to wrap-up, lift, and drive the simulated ball carrier backwards (i.e., tackle).

Equipment Needed: A one-man sled (popsicle).

Description: The players should form a single line, one behind the other, facing the one-man sled at a distance of 10 yards. On the coach's command, the first player in line will run forward, get into a hitting position in front of the sled (popsicle), wrap his arms around the midsection of the popsicle, thrust his hips forward, and drive the sled up to the rear until the coach gives the command to "DROP IT." The next man in line will attack the sled as soon as the coach commands "HIT."

Coaching Points:

- Each player should tackle with a good wrap—with his head up, his eyes open and his neck bowed. The coach can best position himself to observe "closed-eyed tacklers" by standing behind the popsicle, thereby facing the tackler as he approaches the dummy.

- The coach can help develop good tackling techniques by having those who violate the basic techniques of sound tackling (e.g., by ducking their head, closing their eyes, etc.) repeat the drill as often as necessary until they master the required skills.

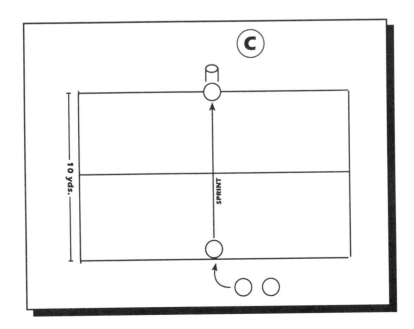

DRILL #52: THE POPSICLE STICK-TAKE DOWN

Objective: To improve the player's ability to wrap-up, lift, drive backwards, and take the simulated ball carrier to the ground (e.g., tackle).

Equipment Needed: A one-man sled (popsicle).

Description: This drill is the same as the previous drill (the "popsicle stick-drive") except that the player will drive the sled into the ground. Again, the players will form a single line, one behind the other, facing the one-man sled at a distance of 10 yards. On the coach's command, the first player in line will run forward, get into a hitting position in front of the sled, wrap his arms around the midsection of the popsicle, thrust his hips forward, and drive the sled up to the rear at an angle until he throws the dummy to the ground. The next man in line will attack the sled after the previous tackler has reset it, and the coach has commanded "HIT."

Coaching Points:

- A good wrap-up tackle involves having the player keep his head up, his eyes open and his neck bowed. (Since a one-man sled weighs approximately 200 pounds, it is recommended that players weighing less than 140 pounds should not participate in this drill for safety reasons).

- The coach can help develop good tackling techniques by having those who violate the basic principles of sound tackling (e.g., by ducking their head, closing their eyes, etc.) repeat the drill as often as necessary until they master the required skills.

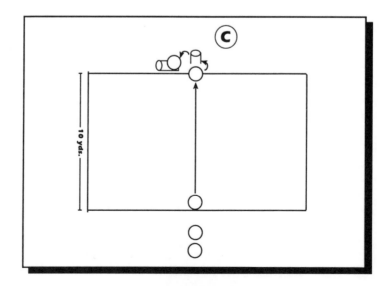

DRILL #53: THE MAT TACKLE

Objective: To improve the player's ability to tackle (wrap-up, lift, drive backwards, and take the ball carrier to the ground), while minimizing the potential for being injured while tackling.

Equipment Needed: A football; a wrestling mat.

Description: This drill can be conducted indoors either without pads or in full pads. Players should be matched in pairs of approximately equal size and weight. One player is designated as a tackler, while the other player serves as a ball carrier. The ball carrier starts the drill by standing with his back to the mat, while the tackler is positioned opposite him at a distance of about 2-3 yards. The coach begins the drill by handing the ball to the ball carrier who stands still and allows himself to be tackled. The tackler accelerates through the runner, while making a good form tackle.

Coaching Points:

- A good wrap-up tackle involves having the player keep his head up, his eyes open and his neck bowed.

- The coach can use this drill to help develop sound tackling techniques in a contact environment that involves little or no chance of injury.

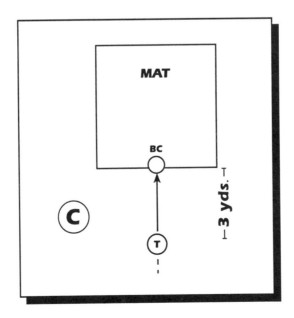

DRILL #54: THE COMPETITIVE DUMMY TACKLE

Objective: To improve a player's ability to tackle; to develop enthusiasm and a competitive spirit; to enhance quickness and reaction time.

Equipment Needed: A dummy; a football; a mat.

Description: Two defensive players should be positioned 10 yards from the mat, positioned on all fours on the ground facing the tackling dummy which stands upright just in front of the mat. The coach begins the drill by moving a football to start the defenders moving. Commands, such as "ROLL RIGHT," "ROLL LEFT," "HIT BELLY" and "HIT," will be used to signal the players to move quickly in the direction indicated and eventually to attack (e.g., tackle) the dummy.

Coaching Points:

- This drill is most effective when participants are divided into teams and score is kept to foster competition between the groups.

- The coach can use this drill to help develop quickness and increase player enthusiasm by balancing teams with players of comparably equal skills.

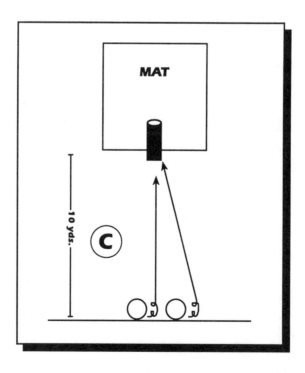

DRILL #55: THE BUTT TACKLE

Objective: To improve the player's ability to "front-up" a ball carrier; to teach a defensive back the proper way to use his eyes, hit while tackling, leverage a ball carrier, and follow through.

Equipment Needed: A football; three to four scrimmage vests.

Description: The drill involves having players work in groups of two—with one acting as a ball carrier and the other as a tackler. The coach positions three to four vests about five yards apart on the line with the two players facing each other at the one end of the line of scrimmage (LOS) at a distance of about 3-4 yards. The drill begins when the coach commands "HIT." The ball carrier moves perpendicular to the LOS and heads for a hole in between the jerseys. While running with the ball carrier, the tackler meets the ball carrier at the LOS with a vigorous "Butt" and a quick wrap without tackling him, which causes the ball carrier to bounce backwards 3-4 yards. The ball carrier then approaches the gap between the next two vests. The tackler repeats his drill sequence of butting and releasing the ball carrier. On his third hit, the tackler finishes the tackle by taking the ball carrier to the ground. The coach then blows the whistle, stops the hitting and rotates new players into position. The direction of the ball carrier's movement (left to right or vice-versa) should also be alternated once each tackler has completed one repetition down the line.

Coaching Points:

- The defenders must get into a good hitting position between each vest, keep their heads up and their eyes open, step into the ball carrier, while using inside-out leverage, and strike a blow with their face and shoulder.

- The tackler should never cross over his feet, get ahead of the ball carrier or drop his head while tackling. The coach can use this drill to review a player's ability to perform all tackling fundamentals properly.

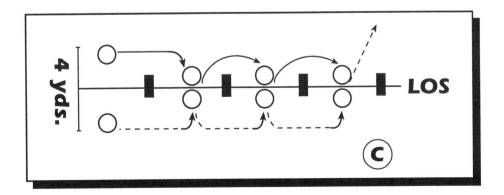

DRILL #56: THE SCORE TACKLE

Objective: To improve the open field tackling ability of the defensive secondary.

Equipment Needed: A football; six scrimmage vests or cones.

Description: The players work in groups of two, with one acting as a ball carrier (BC) and the other serving as a tackler (DB). The coach divides the field into a 6-yard square area, using the cones or scrimmage vests to mark each corner of the square and the middle line which separates Zone A (offensive ball carrier) from Zone B (defensive tackler). The ball carrier starts the drill by moving laterally until the coach commands "SCORE," at which time both players go full speed with the ball carrier trying to score by leaving Zone A, crossing the middle line, eluding the defender and getting across the back line of Zone B. This drill lends itself to score keeping, competition between groups can be fostered depending upon the number of players who are available to engage in the drill.

Coaching Points:

- The point should be emphasized that the defenders should stay in a good hitting position (i.e., never lunging or leaving their feet prematurely). A tackler should keep his head up, his eyes open and "look his lick in" while tackling.

- The tackler should never cross over his feet. He should box the runner in, thereby giving him only one way to go. He should hit from the top of his feet, lock his arms around the ball carrier and drive him backwards.

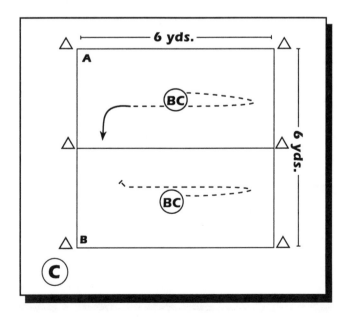

DRILL #57: THE SIDELINE TACKLE

Objective: To improve the ability of defensive backs to tackle in the open field using the sideline as a tackling aide.

Equipment Needed: A football.

Description: The drill involves placing the players in groups of two. One player acts as a ball carrier (BC), while the other is designated as a tackler (DB). The drill starts with both players on a hash mark facing each other about 10 yards apart. The coach begins the drill by tossing the ball (or having someone acting as a quarterback toss the ball to the ball carrier who is simulating a sweep toward the sideline. (Note: The first repetition of this drill can be done at 50-75% speed until both players become accustomed to what is expected.) The designated defensive player takes one step back and out, reads, runs, and then sprints toward the sideline. The tackler approaches the ball carrier diagonally, while maintaining an inside-out relationship. The tackler attempts to give the ball carrier only two choices—run over him or get knocked out of bounds. If the ball carrier tries to cut back, the tackler must correct his leverage and make a heads-up tackle. If the ball carrier continues to the outside, the tackler should butt through him and take him out of bounds. This drill should be repeated using the opposite sideline and rotating players until all players have had one good repetition on each side of the field.

Coaching Points:

- The tackler must stay in a good inside-out hitting position. He must never lunge or leave his feet prematurely. He must keep his eyes open and strike through to the runner's opposite side.

- The tackler should never cross over his feet. He should attempt to box the ball carrier into the boundary, thereby giving him only one way to go.

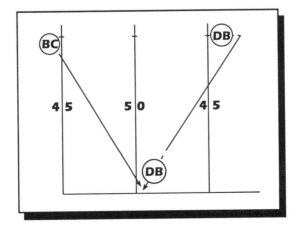

DRILL #58: THE OPEN FIELD TACKLE

Objective: To improve the ability of a defensive player to tackle in the open field.

Equipment Needed: A football; six to eight scrimmage vests or cones.

Description: The coach arranges the field into a 15-18-yard wide tackling area with yard lines marked every five yards. If the field is already marked with the necessary yard lines, then all the coach needs to do is create a 15-yard wide zone with vests or cones. If the field is not marked, then the coach can use cones or vests to mark each corner of each line. The players work in groups of two, with one acting as a ball carrier (BC) and the other as a tackler (DB). (Note: these positions are rotated as the coach deems appropriate.) The ball carrier starts the drill standing in the middle of one end of the tackling area, while the defender assumes a position lined up off to one side at the opposite end of the zone. On the coach's command, "HIT," the defender sprints to the center of the zone, breaks down and prepares to tackle. The coach then throws the ball to the runner. The ball carrier then proceeds toward the tackler. The ball carrier should run hard, avoid going outside the zone, and is allowed only one elusive maneuver (fake). The defensive player should back off the runner when he gets 6-7 yards away from him, await the fake, and commit only after the runner has committed. Because the drill lends itself to score keeping, it can help to develop a spirit of competition between groups of players.

Coaching Points:

- A defender must sprint out, break down and work his feet. He should never allow the runner to get too close to him. He must not take a fake by the ball carrier. He should keep his head up, his eyes open, stay low and work back.

- The ball carrier should not be permitted to use more than one fake. He should make his move, run hard and try to get past the other end of the tackling zone on his feet.

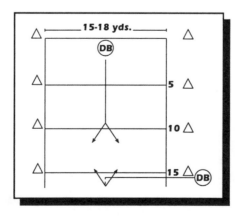

DRILL #59: THE SIDELINE TOWEL TACKLE

Objective: To improve the ability of a defensive back to tackle on the sideline.

Equipment Needed: A football; a towel (or a scrimmage vest).

Description: The coach places a towel or a vest approximately six yards from a sideline. The drill involves pairing the players up. One player serves as a ball carrier (BC), while the other is designated as a tackler (DB). Each pair of players starts the drill by facing each other at a distance of 12-15 yards, ten yards in from the sideline. On the command from the coach to "HIT," the offensive player runs to a point between the towel and the sideline and attempts to make the defensive player miss him. The tackler starts at the same command and approaches at an angle to cut off the runner. The goal of the defensive back is to stop the runner short of the imaginary line between the towel and the sideline. Because this drill lends itself to score keeping, it can be used to foster a spirit of competition between offensive and defensive players.

Coaching Points:

- This drill offers an excellent live, full-speed tackling exercise. It also provides a good opportunity to integrate offensive players on the team into the drill as runners and have them "compete" against the defensive players.

- Both players start the drill at the same time. Points can be based upon who crosses the line first between the towel and the sideline. If the coach wants to foster a sense of competitiveness, he can mandate that the losing player (or group) be required to do push-ups, sit-ups, sprints, etc.

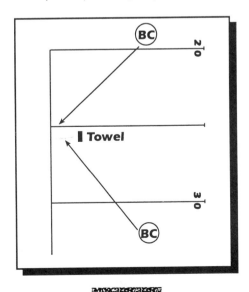

DRILL #60: THE 2-MINUTE TACKLE

Objective: To improve a defender's level of awareness of the game situation; to practice sideline tackling techniques; to enhance the ability of a defensive back to keep a ball carrier in-bounds.

Equipment Needed: A football.

Description: The drill involves pairing up players—one acts as a ballcarrier (BC), while the other serves as a tackler (DB). The players face each other at a distance of 12-15 yards, with the runner on or near the hash mark and the defender positioned approximately ten yards in from the sideline. On the command of the coach to "HIT," the offensive player runs with the ball toward the sideline and attempts to run out of bounds. The tackler, reacting to the same command, approaches at an angle to cut off the runner and attempts to stop the ball carrier short of the sideline. This drill can also be used to foster a spirit of competition between offensive and defensive players by keeping score.

Coaching Points:

- This drill is an excellent way to impress game "sense" upon players. It also provides a good opportunity to integrate offensive players on the team into the drill as runners and have them "compete" against the defensive players.

- Both players start the drill at the same time. Points can be awarded based upon who gets out-of-bounds or is kept in-bounds. If the coach wants to foster a sense of competitiveness, he can mandate that the losing player (or group) be required to do push-ups, sit-ups, sprints, etc.

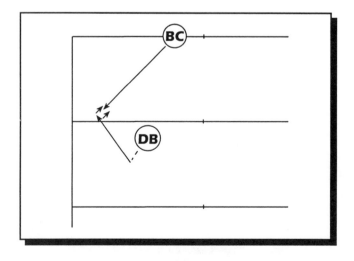

DRILL #61: THE DUMMY STRIP

Objective: To improve the ability of a defensive back to wrap up the receiver and strip the football.

Equipment Needed: A vertical dummy; a wrestling mat.

Description: The players line up, five yards from and facing the coach who stands in front of a mat with a tackling dummy standing on end. On the coach's command "HIT," the defensive back takes a couple of steps backward, recognizes "the receiver on the run with the ball" and accelerates toward the mat. The coach tosses the dummy in the air as the tackler approaches (simulating a wide receiver catching the ball in front of the defensive back). The tackler wraps up the dummy with one arm, while simulating stripping the ball with the other arm. Both the tackler and the dummy should land on the mat. This drill can be performed indoors or outdoors and be done with or without pads, with little fear of someone being injured.

Coaching Points:

- Players should keep their eyes open, drive through the receiver, wrap up and strip the ball simultaneously.

- This drill is a good change-of pace exercise. It provides the opportunity to have a fun, learning experience in the gym on an inclement-weather day.

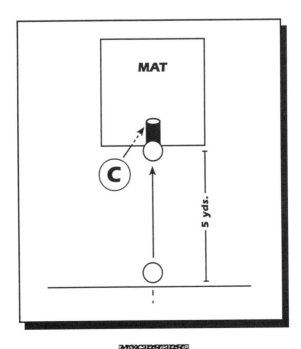

DRILL #62: PURSUIT TACKLING

Objective: To improve the ability of a defensive back to employ a proper pursuit angle on a ball carrier and to make an open field tackle; to develop the ability of a defender to use the sideline when making a tackle.

Equipment Needed: Several footballs.

Description: The drill involves four defensive players who are aligned in their normal four-deep positions and two offensive ball carriers positioned on the LOS approximately two yards inside the sideline. When the coach motions, one of the runners starts running down the sideline. Each defensive back takes a couple of steps backward, recognizes the direction of the run and takes the proper pursuit angle. The coach designates who is to make the tackle (usually one of the defensive backs from the opposite side of the field.) The defensive back selected should use the sideline as a 12th man and make the tackle.

Coaching Points:

- Defenders should never start out pursuing at a flat angle. They should always choose the proper cut-off angle, based upon their speed and that of the runner. This drill should be repeated against offensive backs of varying speed and cutting skills.

- If all defensive backs are required to sprint full speed to the football, this drill can also serve as an excellent conditioning exercise that can be used to replace windsprints.

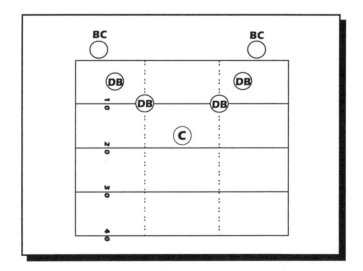

CHAPTER 7

DEFEATING A BLOCK DRILLS

DRILL #63: THE PIANO DRILL

Objective: To improve the ability of a defensive back to play off of a low block.

Equipment Needed: None.

Description: The drill involves six players at a time—one player acts as a defender (DB) while five serve as offensive players (receivers). The drill starts with the offensive players aligned next to each other on a straight line. The coach begins the drill by commanding, "HIT," which is a signal to the first offensive player to attack the defender opposite him by trying to throw a low block at his knees. The defender uses his hands to keep the blocker away from his knees and feet. As soon as the first attempted block is defeated, the defender slides laterally down the line where upon the second blocker immediately attempts to throw the same block against the defender. This sequence continues until all five offensive players have attempted to throw a low block on the defender in rapid succession. The defender finishes the drill by charging past the last man in the line. Subsequently, each player rotated one position to his right (eventually into the defensive position) and the drill is repeated. The players should be given several repetitions on offensive and defense.

Coaching Points:

- The defender should concentrate on the offensive blocker, watching his eyes and timing his arm thrust with the offensive player's block.

- In warding off a block, the defensive player should give ground without allowing the blocker to get to his feet or his knees.

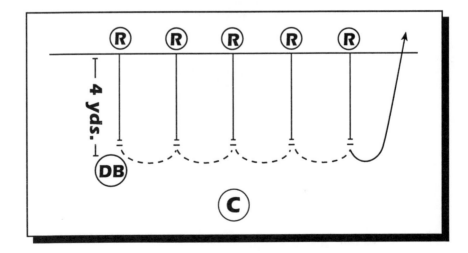

DRILL #64: THE SELL-OUT DRILL

Objective: To improve the ability of a defensive back to defeat or play off of a kick-out block by a fullback or a pulling lineman.

Equipment Needed: A blocking dummy.

Description: The drill involves two players at a time. One player is designated as a blocker ball carrier (BC), while one acts as a defender (defensive back). The coach sets up an offensive line of scrimmage (LOS) behind which he places a blocking dummy 2-3 yards deep in the offensive backfield slightly outside the normal tight end's position. The defensive back is aligned outside the dummy in a normal cornerback's position. Facing him in the backfield is a blocker, at the opposite angle and the same distance from the dummy. When the coach commands, "HIT," or slaps the football, both players will run at the dummy and "sell out," simultaneously hitting on opposite sides of the dummy. The offensive player simulates a kick-out block, as the defender tries to reach the ball carrier after defeating the block. The defender then whips his outside leg into the backfield, causing the ball carrier to lose ground and run laterally, thereby giving pursuing defenders time to catch up with him. It is important to note that if the timing of this drill is "off" (i.e., both players do not arrive at the dummy at the same time), then the defender will simply front-up the ball carrier. At that point, the defender and the blocker-ball carrier will restart the drill until they can "sell out" with a dummy between them.

Coaching Points:

- The defender should drive his inside shoulder through the outside thigh of the blocker (dummy) and "sell out" by doing whatever it takes to break free of the offensive player's block and get to the ball carrier.

- It may take several repetitions before the two players arrive at the impact point simultaneously. If one arrives early and has already knocked the dummy down, the coach should just have them "front up" and start over until they get the timing right.

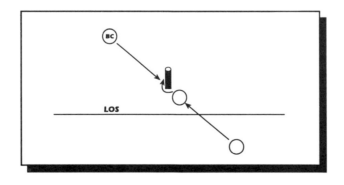

DRILL #65: THE STALK BLOCK—HEAD UP

Objective: To improve the ability of a defensive back to defeat or play off of a head-up stalk block.

Equipment Needed: None.

Description: The drill involves pairing up the players with one player acting as an offensive receiver/blocker (R) and the other as defensive back (DB). The drill begins by having the two participants set up facing each other across a line of scrimmage (LOS) in their normal offensive and defensive alignment and stance (at the coach's discretion). When the coach commands "HIT" or slaps the football, the offensive player attempts to hook the DB straight back in an effort to drive him off of the LOS. The defender tries to get up under the blocker's number, to control him with his hands, and to move him back upfield. The players are then rotated with each getting as many repetitions on offense and defense as the coach believes are appropriate.

Coaching Points:

- The defender should get his hands on the offensive player's numbers and get his head up above the blocker's, pushing him back and toward the inside of the field.

- A defensive back must be strong in his hands and arms. He should work up under the pads of a blocker and through his face in order to control him.

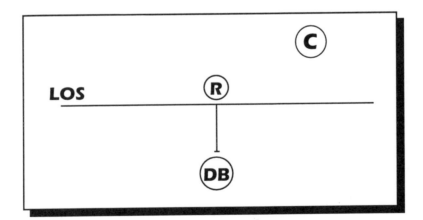

DRILL #66: THE STALK BLOCK-TURN OUT

Objective: To improve the ability of a defensive back to defeat or play off of a turn-out stalk block.

Equipment Needed: None.

Description: The drill involves pairing up the players, with one player acting as the offensive receiver/blocker (R) and the other as a defensive back (DB). The drill begins by having the two participants set up facing each other across a line of scrimmage (LOS) in their normal offensive and defensive alignment and stance (at the coach's direction). When the coach commands "HIT" or slaps the football, the offensive player attempts to block the DB from inside out trying to turn him to the outside of the LOS. The defender tries to get up under the blocker's nearest shoulder pad, working him back toward the center of the field. The players are then rotated with each getting as many repetitions on offense and defense as the coach deems appropriate.

Coaching Points:

- The defender should attempt to get his hands on the offensive player's inside shoulder, while keeping his own arm free to get to the ball.

- The DB must control the blocker and try to force him back toward the football.

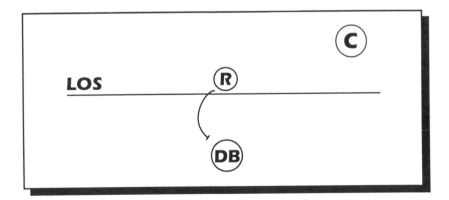

DRILL #67: THE STALK BLOCK-HOOK

Objective: To improve the ability of a defensive back to defeat or play off of a hook stalk block.

Equipment Needed: None.

Description: The drill involves pairing up the players with one player acting as the offensive receiver/blocker (R) and the other as a defensive back (DB). The drill begins by having the two participants set up facing each other across a line of scrimmage (LOS) in their normal offensive and defensive alignment and stance (at the coach's discretion). When the coach commands "HIT" or slaps the football, the offensive player attempts to hook the DB in order to gain the outside position. The defender must attack the blocker's outside shoulder, get up under the blocker's shoulder pads, and move him toward the sideline. The players are continually rotated with each getting as many repetitions on offense and defense as the coach feels are appropriate.

Coaching Points:

- The defender should keep one arm free (preferably his inside arm as he is fighting to get outside with his outside arm). The DB tries to get his hands on the offensive player's outside shoulder in order to push him toward the sideline.

- The DB should try to get the blocker to step too far to the outside, so that he can make a quick step inside (up-and-under move) in order to be better able to get to the ball carrier.

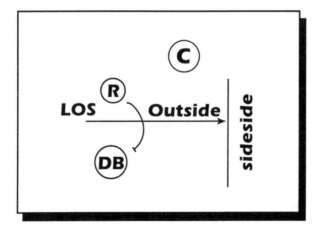

DRILL #68: THE FULLBACK KICK OUT BLOCK

Objective: To improve the ability of a defensive back to defeat or play off of a kick out block by a fullback.

Equipment Needed: None.

Description: The drill involves placing the players in groups of three, with one player acting as the offensive fullback (FB) and two designated as defensive backs (DB). The drill begins by having the three players set up facing each other across a line of scrimmage (LOS) in their normal offensive and defensive alignment and stance (at the coach's discretion). When the coach commands "HIT" or slaps the football, the FB attempts to kick out the DB on that side in order to create a seam between him and the defensive end on that side. The DB must attack the FB at the LOS, striking a blow with his inside forearm and his shoulder pad. The DB should get his feet up under him, and be ready to move upfield or inside.

Coaching Points:

- The defender should be able to fight outside and force wide plays inside without getting too far upfield and creating a gap between himself and the defensive end. The DB must still be able to get back inside and help "up the middle."

- Because fullbacks are usually bigger and stronger than defensive backs, a DB should avoid getting into a contest of strength with them. A DB should use his quickness and speed to get to the ball.

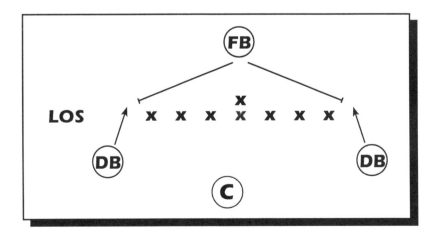

DRILL #69: THE FULLBACK GO UNDER BLOCK

Objective: To improve the ability of a defensive back to defeat or play off of a fullback's block.

Equipment Needed: None.

Description: The drill involves placing the players in groups of three, with one player acting as the offensive fullback (FB) and the other two as defensive backs (DB). The drill begins by having the three players set up facing each other across a line of scrimmage (LOS) in their normal offensive and defensive alignment and stance (at the coach's discretion). When the coach commands, "HIT," or slaps the football, the FB runs to either his left or right side and attempts to kick out the DB on that side. In this situation because the defender knows that he has help to the outside (a rolled-up safety), he attacks at the FB's inside hip and takes him up-field as far as possible. The DB should strike the blow with his outside arm toward the FB's inside shoulder and try to beat him to the inside.

Coaching Points:

- The defender should keep his inside arm free to make the tackle. If the ball goes outside, the defender should force the blocker deep into the ball.

- Because fullbacks are usually bigger and stronger than defensive backs, a DB should avoid getting into a contest of strength with them. A DB should use his quickness and speed to get to the ball and his aggressiveness to make the tackle.

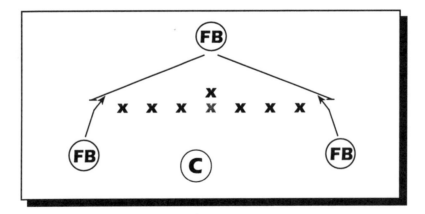

DRILL #70: THE PULLING GUARD BLOCK

Objective: To improve the ability of a defensive back to defeat or play off of a pulling guard's block.

Equipment Needed: None.

Description: The drill involves planning the players in groups of four. Two players act as pulling guards (G), while the other two are designated as defensive backs (DB). The drill begins by having the four players set up facing each other across a line of scrimmage (LOS) in their normal offensive and defensive alignment and stance. When the coach commands "HIT" or slaps the football, the guards pull and attempt to kick out on the DB's. Each defender must play this block just as he would a fullback's block. He attacks the guard, takes him on, bounces back and gets himself under control. He must be able to turn in all wide plays, while helping on inside plays as well. Players should be rotated between offense and defense as the coach feels is appropriate.

Coaching Points:

- The defender should meet the guard as close to the center of the LOS as possible. He must attack under the guard's shoulder pad and force the ball carrier to the inside. If the ball carrier goes to the outside, the defender must try to force the blocker deep into the ball and string the play out to the sideline.

- Because most offensive guards are even bigger and stronger than most fullbacks, defensive backs should avoid getting into a contest of strength with them. A DB should use his quickness and speed to get to the ball and his aggressiveness to make the tackle.

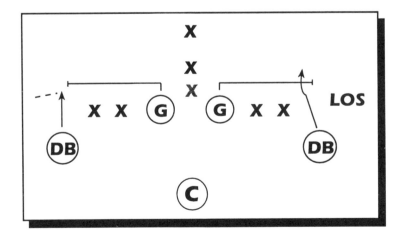

DRILL #71: THE TIGHT END BLOCK

Objective: To improve the ability of a defensive back to defeat or play off of a tight end's block.

Equipment Needed: None.

Description: The drill can be conducted using groups of two players (one side at a time) or four players (both sides of the LOS simultaneously). One defensive back (DB) faces one tight end (TE) on each side of the line of scrimmage (LOS)—each in their normal offensive and defensive alignment and stance (in this case, the DB's are most often strong safeties rolled up in a four deep alignment). When the coach commands "HIT" or slaps the football, the tight ends will attempt to either block the DB on their side or release for a pass. The coach can communicate which option he wants run by either working out hand signals for the offensive player or using a huddle. A defender must read the tight end's release and rapidly determine whether the play is a pass or run. If the play is a pass, the DB must stay "tight" to the TE in pass coverage. If the DB reads run, then he must "face-up" the TE, and be able to turn in all outside running plays, while helping on inside plays as well. Players should be rotated between offense and defense as the coach deems appropriate.

Coaching Points:

- The defender should read the tight end as the TE attempts to release outside. If the DB reads that the play is a run, he should work through the end's face, supporting from the outside in and turning all wide plays inside.

- When the defender reads an "out and up" pass route, he should attempt to knock the TE off of his route in order to throw the TE's timing off. He should also stay with the TE in coverage to the depth desired by the coach.

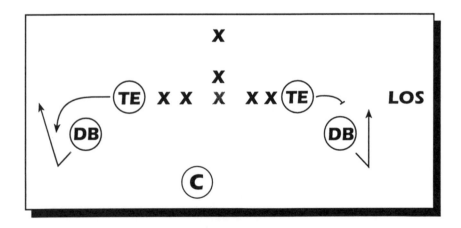

DRILL #72: THE CRACK BLOCK

Objective: To improve the ability of a defensive back to defeat or play off of a wide receiver's crack block.

Equipment Needed: None.

Description: The drill involves two players at a time. One player acts as a defensive back (DB), while the other serves as a wide receiver (WR)—each in his normal offensive and defensive alignment and stance. When the coach commands "HIT" or slaps the football, the WR attempts to crack block the DB. The defender should quickly read the situation and decide upon one of three courses of action. First, he can attempt to beat the block by quickly hitting up-field and forcing the run wide and deep (see Diagram A, below). Second, he can read the crack block and quickly turn his back to the blocker, thereby causing the blocker to clip him (see Diagram B, below). Third, the DB can defeat the crack block by attacking the blocker, driving his inside forearm and shoulder pad through the crack blocker's chest from the inside to outside (see Diagram C, below). All players should be allowed several repetitions at crack blocking and being crack blocked.

Coaching Points:

- The defender should quickly decide which course of action he will take when confronting a crack block—read the crack block, beat it upfield, turn his back and get clipped, or defeat the blocker.

- The DB should not go under or inside a crack block (such a reaction will just make the crack block easy for a blocker). In this instance, a blocker will simply "wall the defender off" thereby allowing the play to make it to the outside. A DB should be smart... read quickly... and act decisively.

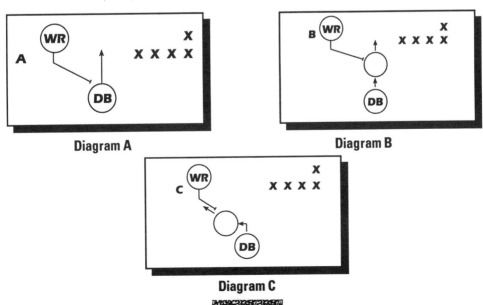

Diagram A

Diagram B

Diagram C

DRILL #73: THE FLARE BLOCK

Objective: to improve the ability of a defensive back to defeat the block of a back flaring out of the backfield.

Equipment Needed: None.

Description: The drill involves placing the players in pairs. One player acts as a defensive back (DB), who is aligned as a rolled-up strong safety or a corner back, facing the other player (designated as a ball carrier), who is coming toward him laterally out of the backfield. When the coach commands, "HIT," or slaps the football, the running back attempts to get an outside position on the DB. The DB must get up field and "take on" the blocker in his path. The DB should drive through the blocker into the path of the pitch man. All players should be rotated between the offense and the defense.

Coaching Points:

- The defender should quickly move into the backfield, drive his inside arm up through the head and neck of the blocker and try to turn the blocker's head upfield. The DB will end up outside, in control and in position to intercept the pitch if the aforementioned steps are executed properly.

- For a change of pace, the DB should attempt to dive over the blocking back. This action has several possible benefits. It may slow the pitch man down, make the pitch man think twice and basically disrupt the timing of the play.

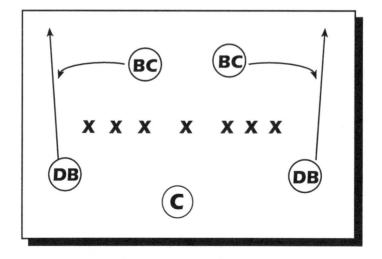

CHAPTER 8

COVERAGE
DRILLS

DRILL #74: LATERAL COVER

Objective: To develop ability of a defensive back to stay with the receiver.

Equipment Needed: None.

Description: The coach has the defensive back stand with his hands behind his back midway between the five-yard lines. A receiver or a running back (BC) then assumes an offensive position, facing the defensive back. On the coach's command, "Go," the offensive player runs laterally, back and forth between the yard lines. The defensive back slides laterally, covering or mirroring the offensive player. After about ten seconds of back-and-forth lateral movement, the coach commands, "Cut," at which time the offensive player turns and attempts to run up-field. The defensive back brings his hands from behind his back and jams the receiver as he attempts to run up-field. He then continues to cover the receiver for about ten yards or until the coach halts the drill.

Coaching Points:

- The coach should require the defensive back to keep his hands behind his back during all lateral movement, and jam the offensive player as soon as possible after the offensive player turns up-field.

- As players become proficient with this drill, the offensive player should run at top speed once he turns up-field as the defensive back attempts to cover him.

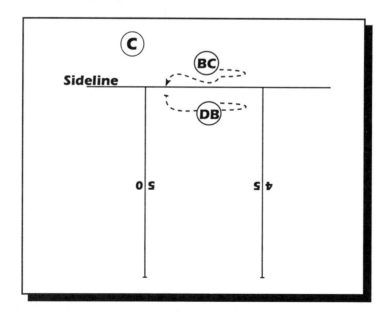

DRILL #75: DEEP COVER

Objective: To develop the ability of a defensive back to cover the receiver going deep.

Equipment Needed: None.

Description: The drill involves pairing up the players. One player acts as a defensive back (DB), while the other serves as a receiver (R). The coach has the defensive back assume a defensive stance, while standing astride one of the yard lines. A receiver then takes up an offensive position about three yards in front of the defensive back, astride the same yard line, facing the defensive back. On the coach's command, "Go," the offensive player runs a weave pattern down the yard line at three-quarters speed, limiting the weave to no more than three yards from the yard line. The defensive back performs this drill with his hands behind his back, staying low and crouched and without crossing his feet. After the defensive back has run about twenty yards, the coach should terminate the drill, have the two players recover and have two other players assume the proper positions to start the drill again.

Coaching Points:

- The coach should require the defensive backs to keep their hands clasped behind their backs throughout the drill and concentrate on not crossing their feet.

- As the defensive backs become proficient at this drill, they should be required to increase both the speed and the distance they must run during the drill.

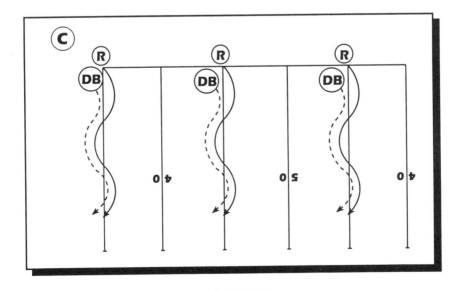

DRILL #76: SPEED TURN

Objective: To develop the ability of a defensive back to cover a receiver who is running a post-corner or a corner-post route.

Equipment Needed: None.

Description: The defensive back assumes a defensive stance five to seven yards in front of and facing the coach. On the coach's command, "Go," the defensive back starts back-pedaling while turning alternately to the inside and the outside, in response to the coach's hand signals. After the player runs back about 15 yards, the coach should give the command, "Break." This is a signal to the player to execute a quick, tight roll or turn to the outside as though covering a braking receiver running a pass pattern. After running about 10 yards past the point when the command "Break" was given, the coach should stop the drill and have the player return to the line of players waiting their turn to run the drill.

Coaching Points:

- The coach should require the players to gradually increase the speed at which they run this drill as they master the techniques involved in the drill.

- Variety and progression can be added to this drill by using a receiver. In this case, either the coach or another offensive player would throw a pass to the receiver after he makes his break on his route to give the defensive back a chance to play the ball.

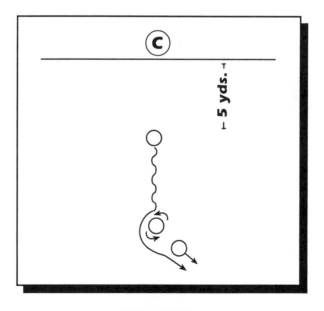

DRILL #77: BUMP AND RUN

Objective: To develop the ability of a defensive back to bump a receiver off his route; to improve the ability of a defensive back to look through a receiver to the ball; to have a defensive back practice continuing to cover his zone after bumping a receiver.

Equipment Needed: A football.

Description: The drill involves pairing up defensive players who alternate being receivers and defensive backs. The receivers line up in a three-point stance with the coach acting as the quarterback. The defensive player lines up in a good defensive stance to cover the receiver. When the coach drops back to pass, the receiver runs either a slant-in or a slant-out route (as directed by the coach). The defensive back lets the receiver get close to him and then gives him a quick, hard bump. If the receiver slants in or runs straight at the defensive player, the defender should bump the receiver's inside shoulder. If the receiver turns out, the DB should bump the receiver's outside shoulder. After the bump by the defender, the coach should throw the football toward the defensive player. Both players should try to catch the ball. Players should alternate receiver and defensive back roles.

Coaching Points:

- The coach should emphasize to the defensive back that he should let the receiver get close to him before bumping him. The defender should not overextend and get off balance when trying to bump the receiver.

- The defensive player should always "look through" the receiver to the quarterback. He should always watch the ball.

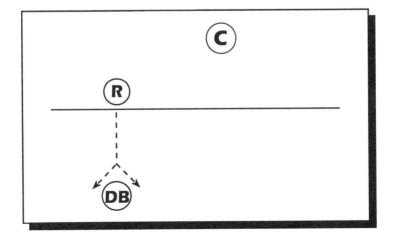

DRILL # 78: THREE-YARD COVER DRILL

Objective: To enhance the ability of a defensive back to be alert to the receiver's movements; to practice being in a comfortable defensive stance; to perfect the start from a defensive stance and to eliminate the false starts and unnecessary steps.

Equipment Needed: A football.

Description: The drill involves pairing up the defensive backs. One player acts as a receiver (R), while the other serves as a defensive back (DB). Depending upon the circumstances, three pairs of players can perform this drill at the same time. The receivers line up about three yards apart in a three-point stance, while defensive backs take up a defensive stance three yards off the receivers. On the coach's movement (the coach drops back with the ball like a quarterback showing pass), the receiver sprints at top speed for approximately ten yards. The defensive back back-pedals, trying not to allow the receiver to get even with him within the 10 yards. After the receivers have run 10 yards, the coach should throw the football toward the center of the defensive players. At that point, both the receivers and the defensive backs all converge on the ball and attempt to catch it. The receivers and defensive backs should then alternate their positions.

Coaching Points:

- The coach should emphasize the importance of a defensive back being alert for the receiver's movements, keeping a low stance and not making false starts or unnecessary steps.

- The difficulty of this drill can be increased by having the defensive backs line up five, seven or nine yards off the receiver and increase the distance the receiver sprints downfield appropriately (i.e., for every two yards deeper the defensive player lines up, the receiver sprints five yards deeper).

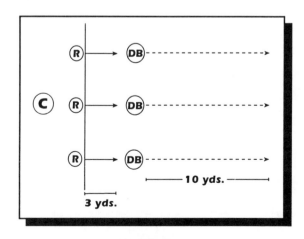

DRILL # 79: COMPETE TO INTERCEPT

Objective: To improve competitive instincts; to enhance interception techniques.

Equipment Needed: A football.

Description: The players form two equal lines facing each other approximately 15 yards apart. One line is designated as offensive players (R), while the other serves as defensive backs (DB). The coach stands to the side of the offensive players and starts the drill by simulating the center snap of the football (slap the ball, bark "hike," etc). The drill begins by having the first player in each line run toward the other player, the coach throws the ball in between the players. The players react to the ball in a one-on-one attempt to catch the football. Once the ball has been caught, the player returns the ball to the coach and the next two players begin.

Coaching Points:

- A defensive player should keep his eyes on the football, protect the ball with his body, and reach the ball as high as possible in the air.

- The coach can control who catches the ball and keep this drill relatively collision-free by where he throws the ball .

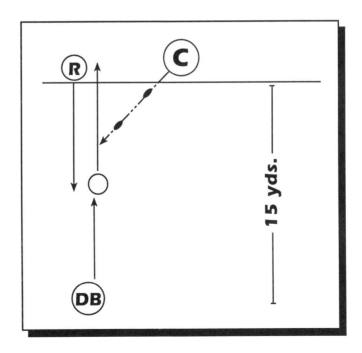

DRILL #80: DEPTH PERCEPTION

Objective: To improve the ability of a defensive back to intercept the longer pass; to increase competitive instincts; to practice a defensive back's interception techniques.

Equipment Needed: A football.

Description: The players form two equal lines facing each other approximately 30-40 yds apart. One line acts as offensive players (R), while the other serves as defensive backs (DB). The coach stands on the sideline with the offensive players and starts the drill by simulating the center snap of the football. The first player in each line runs toward the other at full speed. The coach then throws the ball in between the players approximately 20 yards down the field. The players react to the ball in a one-on-one attempt to catch the football. Once the ball has been caught, the player returns the ball by running it back to the coach and then goes to the end of the opposite line. The coach can help control the competitiveness of this drill and help keep it fairly injury-free by where he throws the football.

Coaching Points:

- The defensive back should keep his eyes on the football, protect the ball with his body, and reach the ball as high as possible in the air.

- Once a defender has intercepted a pass, he should let his teammates know that he has the ball and that they should throw a block for him by hollering a prearranged codeword (e.g., "Fire," "Bingo," etc.).

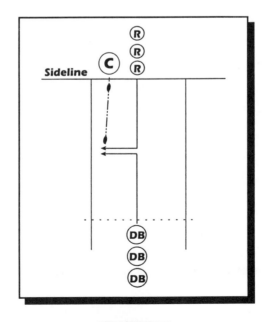

DRILL # 81: DEFENDING THE CURL

Objective: To improve the ability of a defensive back to overtake and step in front of a receiver and intercept the ball without interfering.

Equipment Needed: A football.

Description: The players form a single line facing the coach at a distance of about 20 yards. At the coach's direction, the first two players in line run toward the coach (the first at half-speed, and the second player at ¾ speed). The coach throws the football near the first player (R) at approximately the same time that the second player, (DB) overtakes him. The first player serves as a receiver while the DB second player acts as a defensive back. The intercepting player must step in front of the receiver, intercept the ball without making bodily contact and then return the intercepted ball to the coach. The pair then returns to the end of the line of players. They switch their order in line (defense to offense and vice-versa).

Coaching Points:

- The defender must step around, in front of, or over the shoulder of the receiver without making contact before the ball arrives.

- Once he has intercepted the ball, the defender must keep his eyes on the football until it is under his arm with his hand covering the point of the ball.

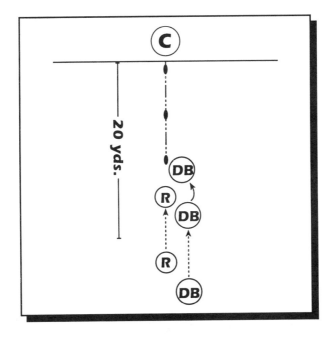

DRILL #82: DEFENDING THE OUT AND UP

Objective: To improve the ability of defensive backs to react to and cover the out-and-up route without getting beat deep.

Equipment Needed: Several footballs.

Description: The drill involves the coach and two players. One player acts as a receiver (R), while the other serves as a corner back (CB), who is positioned in a normal three-deep alignment. The two players line up approximately 10 yards apart. Using signals to the receiver, ("1" finger for an out route and "2" fingers for an out and up route), the coach commences the drill by slapping the football or calling "Set." The defensive back must defend against the out route by always staying on the receiver's outside shoulder. When the number "2" has been called by the coach and the receiver attempts to "Go" downfield, the defensive back should collide with the receiver, knocking him down, out of bounds, or otherwise preventing him from running a "Go" route.

Coaching Points:

- The defender should read the quarterback's (coach's) eyes. The quarterback's eyes will indicate whether he is throwing the out or the out-and-up pass.

- A defensive back should maintain an outside position and react instantaneously to the up or "Go" route. Performing countless repetitions of this drill is an excellent way to master the techniques required to defend against such a pass route.

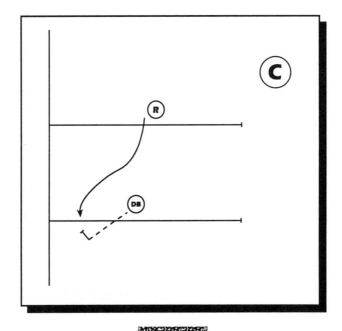

DRILL # 83: THE SPEED TURN

Objective: To improve the ability of a defensive back to cover the post-corner move by a receiver without getting beat deep.

Equipment Needed: Several footballs.

Description: The drill involves pairing up the players. One player acts as a defensive back(DB), while the other player serves as a receiver (R). The two players start this drill approximately 10 yards apart, with the coach and the receiver on the line of scrimmage and the defensive back heads-up on the receiver. The coach commences the drill by slapping the football or calling "Set." The receiver starts to run a post route, which causes the defender to turn and run with him. Once the defensive back has turned, the receiver then turns and runs for the corner. In the process, he crosses the face of the defensive back. The defensive back must then turn his back to the line of scrimmage and sprint to catch the receiver.

Coaching Points:

- The defensive back should read the quarterback's (coach's) eyes while maintaining close proximity to the receiver.

- Instead of crossing over in front of the receiver, the defensive back should roll quickly (i.e., perform a speed turn) and maintain the proper inside and deep position.

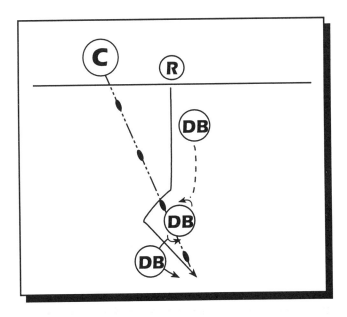

DRILL #84: THE CAT AND MOUSE

Objective: To improve the ability of a defensive back to cover deep routes.

Equipment Needed: Several footballs.

Description: The drill involves pairing up the players. One player acts as a defensive back(DB), while the other serves as a receiver(R). The drill begins with the coach, the defensive back and the receiver on the line of scrimmage. The players line up five yards from the sideline, while the coach is positioned inside the hashmark. The defensive back is facing the receiver, with his back to the coach and his hand on the receiver while he sprints straight downfield on a fly pattern. The defensive back trails the receiver on his inside shoulder, trying to squeeze him into the sideline. Once the receiver has gone 20-25 yards, the coach throws him a pass which both players go for.

Coaching Points:

- The defensive back should read the receiver's head and eyes while maintaining contact with back of the receiver's deepest hand.

- The defender should look back over his inside shoulder, maintaining contact with the receiver and time his move/jump for football once the pass has been thrown.

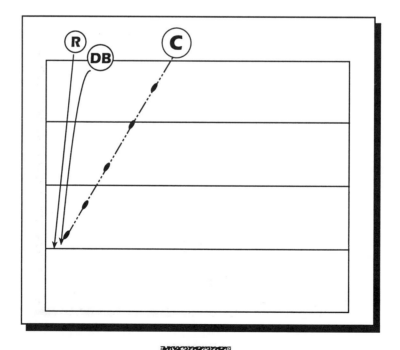

DRILL #85: THE JUMP BALL

Objective: To improve the defensive back's jumping ability, timing and level of competitiveness; to practice "fighting" for the ball.

Equipment Needed: A football.

Description: The drill involves two defenders facing the coach at a distance of about ten yards. The coach throws the ball into the air high enough between the two defenders that both players must leave the ground in order to retrieve the ball at its highest point.

Coaching Points:

- The defensive back must watch the ball, time his leap and fight to get to the highest possible point off of the ground.

- The coach should pair players of similar abilities and repeat this drill at least three times for each pair of defenders.

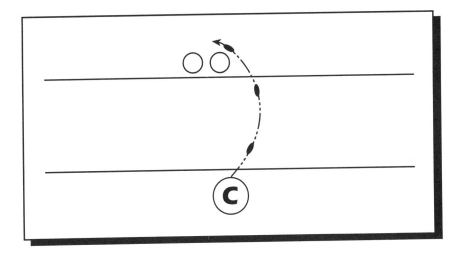

DRILL # 86: THE DOG FIGHT

Objective: To improve the defensive back's timing, level of competitiveness and interception skills.

Equipment Needed: A football.

Description: The drill involves two defenders facing the coach from a distance of 2-3 yards. The coach begins the drill by signaling both players to start back-pedaling, side-by-side. The coach then motions left or right with the football, which is a cue to the defenders to break in the same direction. The coach then throws the ball between the two defensive backs, causing them to fight to get the interception.

Coaching Points:

- The defensive back should watch the quarterback's eyes and the football, while timing his leap and fighting to get to the ball.

- The coach should pair players of mixed abilities and skills and repeat this drill several times for each player until the proper aggressive attitude is exhibited by the defenders.

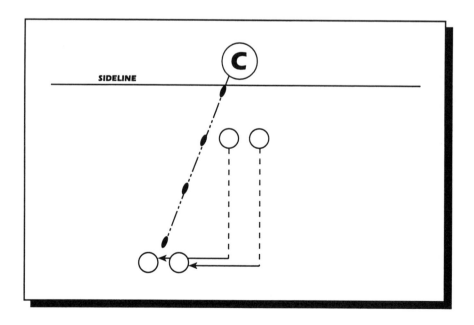

DRILL #87: THE STRIPPER

Objective: To improve the ability of a defensive back to take the ball out of the hands of or "strip" a receiver of the football.

Equipment Needed: A football.

Description: The drill involves pairing up the players. One player acts as a receiver (R), while the other serves as a defender (DB). Each pair lines up facing the coach from a distance of approximately 10-15 yards. The coach assumes a position near the center of the field, with the players 10-15 yards off toward one sideline. On a signal from the coach, both players run toward the center of the field to a point directly opposite the coach. The coach then passes the ball to the receiver. The defender reaches around the receiver with his outside hand trying to dislodge the ball. The players should be given several repetitions from both sidelines, both as a receiver and a defender.

Coaching Points:

- The defensive back should watch the coach's eyes and the football. He should time his strip to dislodge the ball only after the offensive player has touched the ball.

- The defensive back should use his inside arm to keep contact with the receiver. The defender must be prepared to tackle the receiver in case his outside arm does not strip the ball from the receiver's hands.

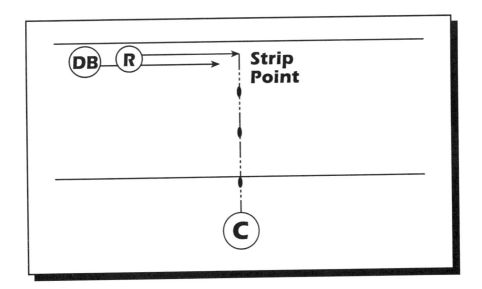

DRILL # 88: BUTT-TO-BUTT STRIP

Objective: To improve the ability of a defensive back to come around the receiver who has already caught the ball and strip it out of his hands.

Equipment Needed: A football.

Description: The drill involves grouping the players in pairs. One player acts as a receiver (R), while the other serves as a defensive back (DB). Each pair lines up with the receiver facing the coach and the defender who has his back to him (butt-to-butt). The pair is positioned 10-15 yards away from the coach. The coach starts the drill by passing the ball to the receiver. No "commands" are used in this drill. The defender reacts to the sound of the receiver's hands hitting the ball by immediately turning around and attempting to strip the ball by pulling on one or both of the receiver's arms. The players should be given several repetitions as both receiver and defender.

Coaching Points:

- The defensive back should listen carefully, react instantaneously to the sound of the football hitting the receiver's hands, time his turn and strip the ball carefully.

- The defender should use his arms to keep contact with the receiver. The defender must be prepared to tackle the defender in case the effort to strip the ball from the receiver's hands is unsuccessful.

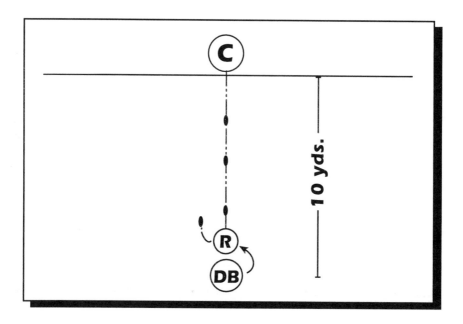

DRILL #89: BUTT-TO-BUTT FIRE

Objective: To improve the ability of a defensive back to react quickly to the call of "Ball" and come around the receiver without making physical contact with him.

Equipment Needed: A football.

Description: The drill involves grouping the players in pairs. One player acts as a receiver (R), while the other serves as a defensive back (DB). The players assume a position ten yards in front of the coach. The receiver faces the coach, while the defender has his back to the receiver. To begin the drill, the coach throws the ball to the receiver. When the ball gets to within three yards of the receiver, all of the defensive backs who are not currently participating in the drill yell "Ball." The defender then snaps around in front of the receiver without making contact with him. He looks for the ball, intercepts it, and returns it to the coach.

Coaching Points:

- The defensive back should listen carefully, react instantaneously to the call, and time his effort to move and intercept the ball without making physical contact with the receiver carefully.

- To increase the level of difficulty of this drill, the coach can require the defender to snap over the right side of the receiver while he throws the ball to the outside left of the receiver.

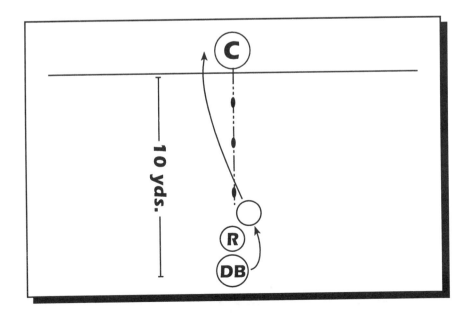

DRILL # 90: TIP AND BLOCK

Objective: To improve the ability of a defensive back to transition rapidly from defense to offense and block potential tacklers.

Equipment Needed: A football; a blocking dummy.

Description: The drill involves grouping the players in pairs. Both players act as defenders. Each pair lines up with the first player (P-1) facing the coach from a distance of approximately 10 yards away with a blocking dummy beside him. The second player (P-2) assumes a position on a line facing the coach at a distance of approximately 20 yards. The coach starts the drill by passing the ball to the first defensive back who tips the ball back over his head to the second defender. The deepest defender intercepts the ball, hollers a command (e.g., "BINGO"/ "GO" / "FIRE," etc.) and runs the ball back to the coach. As soon as the first player hears the "codeword," he blocks the dummy who represents a potential receiver (formerly on offense, now on defense.) Players should be given several repetitions as both the first and second man in line.

Coaching Points:

- The first defender should tip the ball high, listen and block the "dummy" at the waist.

- The second defender should catch the ball at its highest point, yell the transition-to-offense codeword loudly enough that all teammates can hear and sprint the ball back to the coach.

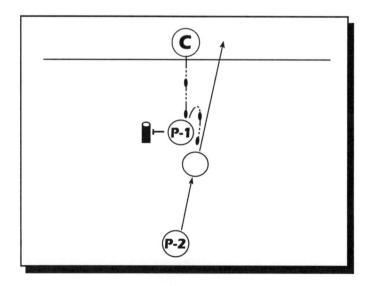

DRILL #91: TEAM TIP

Objective: To improve the ability of a defensive back to concentrate on the ball at all times; to practice keeping the ball in play.

Equipment Needed: A football.

Description: The coach has the players form a single line, with about two yards between each player. The first player (P-1) in line should be approximately 20 yards away from the coach, facing him. When the coach raises the football showing pass, the first player in line runs toward the coach. After the player runs a few yards, the coach throws a high pass to the player. The player does not catch the ball, but tips it up in the air to the second player (P-2), who will likewise tip the ball to the third player (P-3), and so on. The last player in line catches the ball and tosses it back to the coach. The players then line up again, with the second player moving to the first player position, the previous first player moving to the end of the line, etc. The coach should continue this drill until all players have had the chance to be in the first-player position.

Coaching Points:

- The coach should emphasize the importance of everyone keeping their eyes on the ball.

- The coach should establish as a basic goal that each player tips the football to the player behind him and that the last player in line must catch the ball without letting it hit the ground.

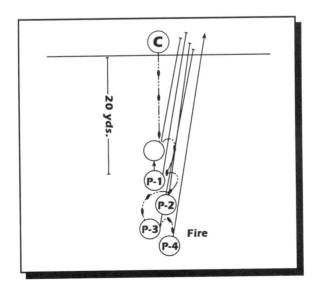

DRILL # 92: REACT AND ACCELERATE

Objective: To improve the ability of a defensive back to read the quarterback's movements, react quickly and intercept the football.

Equipment Needed: Several footballs.

Description: The drill involves having players line up three abreast approximately 15-20 yards away from the coach. The middle player acts as a defender (DB), while the two outside players serve as receivers (R). The coach starts the drill by commanding "Set." He then slaps the ball and turns his shoulders and steps toward one of the two receivers. The defender reacts to the coach's (quarterback's) body movement by sprinting toward the receiver on the indicated side of the field. When he gets within a yard or two of the receiver, the coach passes the ball to that receiver, causing everyone in the group to call "BALL." The defender then lifts his head quickly, locates the football and intercepts the ball. Players should each be given several opportunities to be the "man in the middle".

Coaching Points:

- The middle man must watch the coach's (quarterback's) front foot which will indicate to him which direction he should go.

- The first move of the defender should be a heads-down sprint to his left or right, followed by a heads-up search for the football. When the interception is made, the defender should call out the codeword and sprint the ball back to the coach.

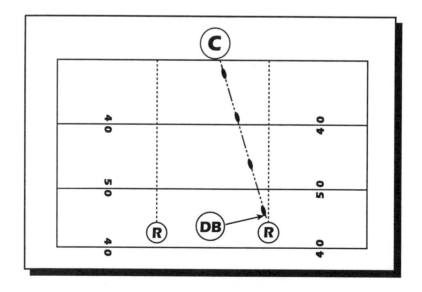

DRILL # 93: 2-ON-1 VERTICAL STRETCH

Objective: To improve the ability of a defensive back (a 2-deep safety) to protect his zone against an equal vertical stretch by two wide receivers, react quickly and intercept the football.

Equipment Needed: A football.

Description: The drill involves having a defensive back (DB) align himself 10 yards away from and facing the coach in the middle of the held. Two players, acting as receivers (R), position themselves beside the coach an equal distance on either side of the defender (about a yard outside hashmark). The coach starts the drill by commanding "Set." He then slaps the ball, which is a signal to each receiver to sprint straight down the field. The defensive back must back-pedal, all the while keeping his eyes on the coach (quarterback). He must never allow either receiver to get behind him. When the coach (quarterback) turns to throw the ball to one of the receivers, the defender reacts by sprinting toward an interception point. When the interception is made, the defender calls out the codeword and sprints the ball back to the coach. Players are then rotated so that each has several opportunities to be both the defender and the receiver.

Coaching Points:

- The defensive back should watch the coach's (quarterback's) eyes while keeping both receivers in front of him by using peripheral vision.

- The receivers should just keep running straight down the field. Once the ball has been thrown they should not go for the football in order to prevent collisions and possible injuries.

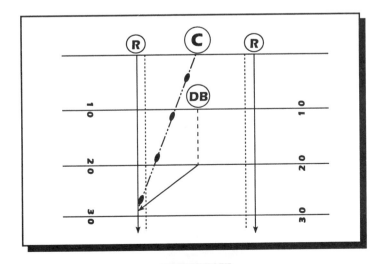

DRILL #94: THE HASH MARK DRILL

Objective: To improve the ability of a defensive back to cover the area between the hashmarks; to practice reacting to a thrown ball and intercepting the football.

Equipment Needed: A football.

Description: The drill involves having a defensive back (DB) align himself 10 yards away from and facing the coach in the middle of the field. Two other players, acting as receivers (R), align themselves beside the coach an equal distance on either side of the defender (about a yard outside hashmarks). The coach starts the drill by commanding "Set." He then slaps the ball and begins to drop back to pass, which is a signal to each receiver to sprint straight down the field. In reaction to the situation the defensive back must back-pedal, while keeping his eyes on the quarterback and the receivers. He must not allow either receiver to get behind him. At that point, the coach yells "Hook," which is a prearranged signal to one of the receivers to stop and run a hook pattern inside the hashmark. Simultaneously, when the coach (quarterback) turns to throw the ball to one of the receivers. The defender then reacts to the flight of the ball by sprinting toward an interception point. When the interception is made, the defender calls out the codeword and, sprints the ball back to the coach. Players are then rotated so each has several opportunities to be both the defender and the receiver.

Coaching Points:

- The defensive back should watch the coach's (quarterback) eyes while maintaining the proper depth and cushion. He must react quickly once the ball is thrown by sprinting to the interception point.

- This drill should be performed at full speed with the defender running full speed through the receiver to the football. The coach should also vary the depth to which he throws the football to give the defensive back the opportunity to cover all the distance between the hash marks.

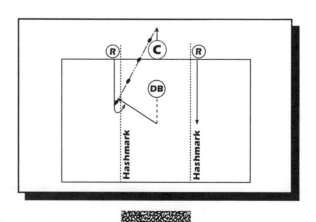

DRILL # 95: COVER DOWN

Objective: To improve the ability of a defender to break on the ball once it is thrown, react quickly and intercept the football; to practice tipping the ball.

Equipment Needed: A football.

Description: The coach acting as the quarterback, throws against a normal 3-deep, 4-deep or full defensive alignment. The coach begins the drill by commanding "Set." He then slaps the ball to start the defenders moving in response to the football (i.e., the coach moves the ball to the left—the defenders slide right, etc.) The coach then throws the ball at any one of his defensive backs. Each defender is required to tip the ball into the air without intercepting it. As soon as the defenders know where the ball has been thrown, they sprint to that area. The second player must also tip the ball, followed by the third player, and so on. Finally, the last player in line intercepts the ball, yells the codeword for an interception, and returns the ball to the coach.

Coaching Points:

- The defenders should watch the coach's (quarterback's) eyes, sprint to the ball, tip it in the air and beat the interceptor back to the line of scrimmage.

- The last man to touch the ball leaps, intercepts the ball, and runs the ball back to the coach.

- This drill should be repeated if the ball hits the ground or if any of the players who tipped the ball do not cross the line of scrimmage before the defender who intercepted the ball.

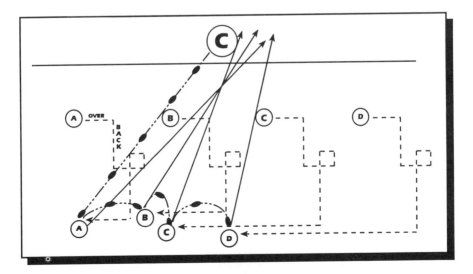

DRILL # 96: PASS PURSUIT

Objective: To improve the ability of a defensive back to get quickly to his drop area using the proper pursuit angle; to practice reacting to intercepting the football.

Equipment Needed: A football.

Description: The coach, acting as the quarterback, throws against a normal 3-deep, 4-deep or full defensive alignment. The coach begins the drill by commanding "Set." He then slaps the ball to start the defenders moving in response to the football. The coach uses a straight drop-back pass to evaluate whether all portions of the defensive backfield are properly covered. To keep the defenders honest, however, he incorporates a few running plays into his simulated attack. Once the coach throws the ball at any one of his defensive backs, all of the other players participating in the drill should sprint to a position in front of the player who intercepted the ball, holler the codeword and simulate blocking downfield to escort the interceptor into the endzone. The defender who intercepted the ball returns the football to the coach.

Coaching Points:

- The defenders should watch the coach's (quarterback's) eyes, sprint to the area where the ball was thrown, and beat the interceptor back to the line of scrimmage.

- The coach should evaluate and correct the defensive coverage, movement to coverage, pursuit angles, team hustle, etc.

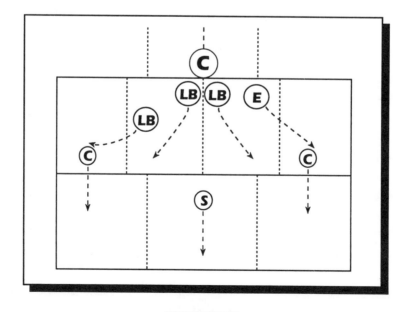

DRILL # 97: THE MIRROR SCORE

Objective: To improve the ability of the defensive backs to use one-on-one coverage; to practice keeping an offensive man from crossing the line of scrimmage.

Equipment Needed: Two cones or scrimmage vests.

Description: Two players face each other at a distance of one yard. One player acts as a ballcarrier (BC), while the other acts as a defender (DB). The coach sets up two cones or vests 2-3 yards apart on a line between the players. The coach starts this drill by commanding "HIT." This is a signal to both players to sprint forward toward the line. The defensive player uses both hands and attempts to keep the offensive player from getting both of his feet over the line. The offensive player has 20 seconds to get both of his feet across the line as many times as possible. The players' roles are then reversed in order to provide both players with the opportunity to perform the drill on each side of the line. The winner is the player who allows the offensive player to cross the line the least number of times.

Coaching Points:

- The defender should concentrate on his man. He should maintain his position and never lunge or leave his feet prematurely. He should keep his eyes open and strike through the numbers of the offensive player, putting his hands under the offensive player's shoulder pads.

- The ball carrier should not run too low. He should keep in mind that his goal is to get both of his feet across the line as many times as possible within 20 seconds. If he is knocked to the ground, he gets only one point and loses valuable time.

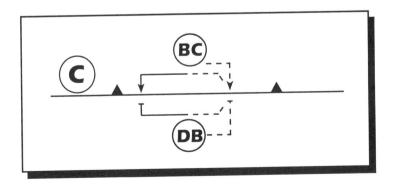

DRILL #98: BUMP THE RECEIVER

Objective: To improve the ability of a defensive back to knock a receiver off of his route.

Equipment Needed: None.

Description: The drill involves two players at a time. One acts as a receiver (R), while the other serves as a defender (DB) who is covering an outside zone. The coach starts this drill by commanding " HIT " or slapping a football. The offensive player then sprints downfield at the defender and attempts to release to the inside or outside. The defender allows the receiver to get close enough to him to bump him and attempts to knock him off his pass route. The defender should hit the outside shoulder of the receiver if the receiver comes at him or releases inside. The defender should hit the receiver's inside shoulder if the receiver attempts to release outside. After a predetermined number of repetitions, the players' roles are reversed in order to provide both players the opportunity to play on both offense and defense.

Coaching Points:

- The defender should concentrate on the receiver and the quarterback simultaneously (look through the receiver to the ball). The defensive back should allow the receiver to get close and then give him a good bump, without the DB lunging or losing his balance.

- The defensive back should not try to reach too far for the receiver. He may get overextended and lose him. A defender must be able to read whether the play is a run or a pass.

- Variety can be added to the drill by incorporating a quarterback into the drill and having him throw a pass to a receiver, who must be defended "live" by a defensive back.

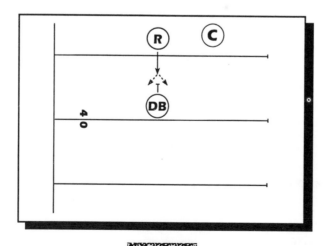

CHAPTER 9

FUMBLE RECOVERY DRILLS

Drill 99: Fumble Recovery

Objective: To teach defensive backs the proper method of falling on a loose football.

Equipment Needed: A football.

Description: A ball is placed three to four yards in front of a defender. On command, the defensive back dives forward and reaches out to the ball. On contact, the defender pulls the ball to his stomach and curls around the ball, lying on his side to protect himself.

Coaching Point:

- Variety and competition can be added to the drill by using one ball per two (or more) lines and having two (or more) players go for a fumble recovery simultaneously.

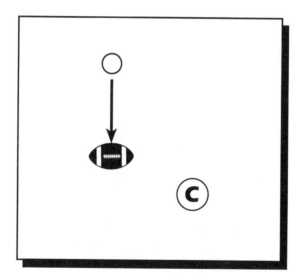

Drill # 100: Loose Ball Fumble Recovery

Objective: To practice going after a loose football; to develop hand and eye coordination

Equipment Needed: A football.

Description: The coach has the defensive backs form one line about 20 yards from him and facing him. When the coach raises the football showing pass, the first player in line sprints toward him. When the player is within 10 yards of the coach, the coach should throw the football at the ground several yards in front of the oncoming player (the coach should try to make the football hit the ground so it takes some wild bounces—i.e., release the ball sideways so that it knuckles). The player should concentrate on keeping his eye on the moving ball and retrieve the "fumble." The player should then toss the ball back to the coach and return to the end of the line. The coach then raises the football again to start the next player in the drill, and so on.

Coaching Points:

- The coach should emphasize the importance of getting control of the ball before attempting to pick it up and run with it.

- The coach should instruct the players to fall on the ball to make sure of the recovery if they are having trouble gaining control of the ball.

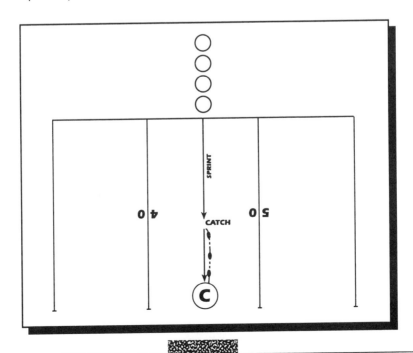

Drill #101: Fight for it Fumble Recovery

Objective: To teach defensive backs to fight for a loose ball.

Equipment Needed: A football.

Description: Two defenders line up alongside each other. On command, the defensive backs fall forward, touch their chests to the ground, and scramble after a ball that has been thrown between them.

Coaching Point:

- The coach should instruct the defender to pull the ball to his stomach on contact and curl around it.

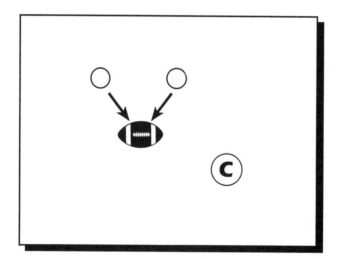

Ron Dickerson Sr. is the head football coach at Temple University, a position he assumed in late 1992. Since assuming the reins of the Owls' gridiron program, Dickerson has led a concerted effort to turn around Temple's football fortunes. Prior to accepting his first head position at Temple, Dickerson served as the defensive coordinator at Clemson for two years. In his two seasons on the Tigers' staff, Dickerson helped Clemson boast one of the nation's toughest and best defensive units.

A 1971 graduate of Kansas State University where he had a distinguished football career, earning three letters as a cornerback for the Wildcats, Dickerson began his coaching career at his alma mater in 1972 after an injury-shortened stint as an NFL player. He served as KSU's secondary coach for four seasons (1972-'75), before moving on to the University of Louisville for three years in the same position. Other stops in Dickerson's coaching career include the University of Pittsburgh (1978-'80), the University of Colorado under head coach Bill McCartney (1982-'84), and Pennsylvania State University on Joe Paterno's staff (1985-'90).

Ron and his wife of 29 years, Jeannie, have two children—son Ron Jr. and daughter Rashawn.

James A. Peterson, Ph.D., is a free-lance writer. A 1966 graduate of the University of California at Berkeley, Peterson served on the faculty of the United States Military Academy at West Point for 16 years. A prolific writer, Peterson has written or co-authored 43 books and more than 150 published articles. A Fellow of the American College of Sports Medicine, he has appeared on several national television shows, including ABC's Good Morning America, The CBS Evening News, ABC's Nightline, and The Home Show. He and his wife of over 29 years, Susan, reside in Monterey, California.

ADDITIONAL FOOTBALL RESOURCES FROM

TITLES FROM THE 101 DRILLS SERIES

O F F E N S E

101 Quarterback Drills
Steve Axman
1998 ▪ 128 pp ▪ Paper ▪ ISBN 1-57167-191-9 ▪ $16.95

101 Ways to Run the Option
Tony DeMeo
1999 ▪ 140 pp ▪ Paper ▪ ISBN 1-57167-368-7 ▪ $16.95

101 Receiver Drills
Stan Zweifel
1998 ▪ 128 pp ▪ Paper ▪ ISBN 1-57167-191-9 ▪ $16.95

D E F E N S E

101 Linebacker Drills
Jerry Sandusky and Cedric X. Bryant
1997 ▪ 120 pp ▪ Paper ▪ ISBN 1-57167-087-4 ▪ $16.95

101 Defensive Line Drills
Mark Snyder
1999 ▪ 120 pp ▪ Paper ▪ ISBN 1-57167-372-5 ▪ $16.95

TO PLACE YOUR ORDER OR FOR A FREE CATALOG:
U.S. customers call
TOLL FREE: (800) 327-5557
or visit our website at
www.coacheschoice-pub.com
or FAX: (217) 359-5975
or write
COACHES CHOICE™
P.O. Box 647, Champaign, IL 61824-0647